How to Make $2000 a Week Selling Information by Mail

by

Russ von Hoelscher

How to Make $2000 a Week Selling Information by Mail

by

Russ von Hoelscher

Dedicated to those men and women who are both dreamers and doers. Very special people who believe in the free enterprise system, and who want to make more money and enjoy more of the good life.

ISBN: 0-940398-26-5

TABLE OF CONTENTS

Your time is money—use it wisely!

INTRODUCTION

I began my mail order career over 20 years ago. I'm still in it, bigger and better than ever, and I'm still convinced it's one of the most personally satisfying and profitable businesses of them all.

I've sold hundreds of products and services for myself and others, by mail—everything from candy to candles, and from sensual lingerie to a Texas cattle ranch. Almost any worthwhile product or service, if it's at all unique, can be sold by mail. However, many years ago I realized that one product stood head and shoulders above all others. In a word that product is:

INFORMATION

Information packaged in the form of books, manuals, reports, newsletters, audio or video tapes, etc., is the ideal mail order product. Good, up-to-date information is always in demand. Subject matter is almost unlimited; it can be easily packaged, printed, sold, and shipped. Even in a time of high postage costs, the United States Postal Service allows substantial discounts to purveyors of published matter.

Let me help you carve out a nice big chunk of the profit pie. *First you learn, then you earn!* Yes! You can easily make $400 a day, $2,000 a month, and up to $100,000 per year, and more, in this fascinating business. You can start in your spare time at home, with only a small investment. If you have desire, are dedicated and persistent, you can build this business into something exciting and grand.

Best of all, you'll find this exciting business to be a true joy. You'll hit the floor running every morning, and hurry home from your regular job at night. You'll know the exhilaration of building your own business and watching it steadily grow bigger and better. You will control your own financial destiny!

Writing, publishing, distributing and mail order bookselling have provided me with a first-class lifestyle (the nice homes, big fancy cars, dream vacations) over the years, and I'm eager to share this goldmine of knowledge with you.

Here is a super business opportunity for you, with true, get-rich potential. Oh, no, it's not another hair-brained get-rich-by-next-Thursday scam. The woods are full of silly, unworkable get-rich schemes, but I have never been involved in such unethical flim-flam. I want you to know who I am, and what I stand for, *does* make a difference. When I present a money-making opportunity, it's the real thing. And, I consider the topic of this book—selling books and other forms of information by mail—to be today's Number One wealth-building opportunity.

I want you to read this book carefully. Although small in size, this book can be an indispensable tool that flings open the door to a financially free future for you.

You deserve Total Success,

Russ von Hoelscher

Russ von Hoelscher

6

I've been broke, but I have never been poor. Rich and poor are both states of mind. Take my advice: **think rich!**

—Russ von Hoelscher

10
9
8
7
6
5
4
3
2
1
·
BLAST OFF!

"*Begin. To begin is half the work.*"
—Ausonius

WHY MAIL ORDER?

Modern mail order is a powerful sales medium that offers unlimited moneymaking potential for today's entrepreneur. Best of all, you can get started part-time, at home, and with a small investment!

The joy of mail order! Almost everyone loves to receive mail—personal mail and business mail. It's fun to open letters from far-off places and check out the contents. Now imagine opening a huge stack of letters filled with cash, checks and money orders and you will understand one main attraction of the mail order business. Another big attraction is that you can launch a home-based mail order book business with only limited cash to invest. Many of today's successful mail order tycoons made a successful start with very small start-up capital. Modern mail order allows you to start small and build a business with unlimited profit potential.

How Much Capital is Required?

Mail order is one of the few businesses left in which you can make a "kitchen table" shoestring start. Obviously, some start-up capital is required to place advertising or make mailings. However, you can decide your own level of financial commitment. A small (to begin with) home-based mail order business can be launched with very limited expenses. Many successful mail order operators have launched their business with only a few hundred dollars in initial expense.

Getting Started

A home-based mail order book business can literally be started from the kitchen table. Many operators started in just that way, before proceeding to "more businesslike quarters" in the home or an outside office.

When the kitchen table offers the only necessary space, use it. However, if at all possible, search out other areas of your house or apartment that offer more privacy. Your own home office or a spare bedroom that can be converted to office space is ideal. Even open space in a garage may serve your initial start-up needs.

Basic Supplies and Equipment

1. a desk and chair
2. file cabinet
3. envelopes, letterheads, and other printed matter
4. typewriter
5. storage area/folding table
6. miscellaneous office supplies (rubber bands, paper clips, envelope openers, glue, typewriter correction liquid, etc.)
7. a large wastebasket
8. proper lighting
9. postage stamps

10. checking account
11. a bookkeeping system
12. telephone

You may, of course, improvise. Any table, including the kitchen table, may serve as your desk during your initial start. However, do get yourself a real desk, even if it is a used one from the Goodwill or Salvation Army, as soon as you can. Your own desk will give you a more positive feeling of "being in business for yourself." Likewise, you could use a spare closet or your own bookshelves in place of a file cabinet at first, but again, purchase a sturdy four-drawer file cabinet as soon as possible.

It is almost impossible to do business without using a typewriter. You can either buy one second-hand or rent a nice model by the month at reasonable rates. If you can't even "two-finger type," a typing course at a local adult education school should have you pecking away in good order, and these classes usually charge very low tuition. If you are married or live with someone with office skills, they can be of real help to you.

Don't underestimate the importance of adequate lighting. Also, purchase a large, comprehensive journal at an office supply store and get started right by keeping good business records. Your record-keeping is vital. It will tell you in which direction your business is heading. A separate checking account for your mail order business is important. Make notations as to what every check went for (supplies, advertising, rentals, etc.) and this will assist you in keeping good records.

You also need a phone on or near your desk or work area. It may be called the mail order business, yet you will still find yourself using the telephone often to order supplies, obtain information, etc. You may or may not wish to use your own phone number in your ads, catalogs and circulars going to your customers. Some mail order sellers do, with satisfactory results· others prefer that all business be done by mail. If you use only a postal box as your address, I feel a phone number is helpful. People like to do business with individuals or firms who appear to be accessible.

Where You're Located

When you first start a mail order business, your business location will most likely be your house or apartment. Later, when your business grows, you may wish to rent an office outside your home. To conserve money, it is wise to start right at home. Fact is, many veteran information by mail sellers continue to do business in their homes, even after achieving great success. This is the age of information, and it's also a fact—more and more people are discovering the many advantages of living and working in the same place—home, sweet home.

In the beginning, you won't need a lot of space to launch your business. Later, when more room is needed, you'll have to either rent office and warehouse space, or if you prefer to continue to do business from your home, you can rent mini-storage space at one of the thousands of self-contained storage rental centers that are now found almost everywhere.

Your mailing address can be your home address, a post office box, or a private mail drop. Thousands of private mail centers have opened in recent years, and they offer entrepreneurs a choice between using their home address—not too good an idea in an all residential area, especially if you don't want potential local customers knocking on your door—and a post office box (there are still some people who believe a street address adds more stability than a postal box). Many of the private mail centers will let you use their street address and then assign you a box number to go with it. In some cases, you can substitute a "Suite" number for the box number.

Listed below are examples of all three options, and how they'll look. You decide which one you like.

Mail Order Marketing
2909 Rice Street
Your City, State, Zip

Mail Order Marketing
P.O. Box 1090
Your City, State, Zip

Mail Order Marketing
500 Market St., Suite 302
Your City, State, Zip

Obviously, your home address will add no extra cost. A post office box is most reasonable, from $20 to $50 per year, according to the size of the box rented. A private mail center will cost considerably more. At between $10 and $18 per month, on the average, your yearly rate will be in the $120 to $200 range.

Who is Qualified?

Almost anyone of average intelligence with a true desire for success is more than qualified to begin a mail order business.

BUSINESS PEOPLE—Any businessman, or woman, will already possess most of their basic knowledge and skills to operate a mail order venture.

SALES PEOPLE—Many men and women active in sales, either to business or consumers, have launched successful mail order selling careers, either part-time or full-time. Their knowledge of what makes people "buy" can greatly aid them in mail order selling.

HOUSEWIVES—A part-time mail order business can liberate the housewife who is bored and has extra, unproductive hours on her hands. In years past, mail order was a "man's business," but the 1970s and 1980s saw many thousands of women get involved in mail order selling. You can expect to see this trend continue and grow throughout the 1990s, and beyond.

RETIRED PEOPLE—It has been estimated that over 25% of the one-person or one-couple mail order firms are run by semi-retired folks. A home-based mail selling second career can have a rejuvenating effect on senior citizens who find themselves with too much leisure time. By becoming active in mail order, many seniors earn needed extra income and may even extend their life span by building their self-esteem through business activity.

THE WHOLE FAMILY—The Donovans of Milwaukee, Wisconsin, launched a mail order business a few years ago that involved the whole family. Mr. and Mrs. Donovan and their two teenage girls and one pre-teenage boy have manufactured and sold homemade kites by mail. Joe Donovan says that the home mail order business brought the family closer together than anything else ever had. Good enough reason for others to consider total family involvement in a home-oriented business.

For the record, the Donovans recently became one of our super *Profit Ideas* "FAST START" booksellers. Although they still sell kites, Joe says, "Eventually, I expect the book-selling business to eclipse the kite business in sales and profitability. And there sure is less hassle and product damage in selling books by mail."

Amen!

What's in a Name?

Don't choose your company name in a haphazard fashion. The name you hang on your new fledgling firm could be a liability or an asset. It can help entice orders or turn potential customers off.

14

Many new mail order dealers simply use their own name. If it is your name, it need not be registered, which is required by most states when fictitious names are used. Although this practice works for some, often it is wiser to use a company name that is either catchy or gives a better description of the products you sell.

The late, great mail order genius, Joe Karbo, earned millions using his own name to sell his famous classic, *The Lazy Man's Way to Riches*. Using his own name fit perfectly with the kick-back, "Lazy Joe" image his ad copy was conveying. Ben Suarez took just the opposite approach in his road to fortune. Selling books from his own home, he gave his new company a grand name—The Publishing Corporation of America! And when he was selling over a million of his "Life-Luck Horoscopes," he created the perfect name to market the horoscopes—The International Astrological Association. Now, think about it! Wouldn't you feel better about ordering astrology items from The International Astrological Association than in placing your order to just a person's name? Keep this in mind when you pick a name to do business with. In some cases, your own name may do fine; in others, you can give yourself a powerful image by selecting a name that fits well with the product or service you sell.

If your name is John Smith, you have every right to sell books, or other products, using your legal name. However, you just may find that names such as *Smith Opportunity Book Company*, or simply, *Opportunity Book Marketplace*, gives a greater impression regarding size, stability, etc., to the mail order-buying public. We never should try to deceive our customers, but if our business name makes us appear to be a larger firm than we really are, no harm done. It's not a good practice to announce to the world that we are small, new and "green" to mail order.

Obtaining a D.B.A.
and/or a Business License

In most cities and towns, you will need a "d.b.a." (doing business as) if you use a name other than your own. Also, most municipalities require all types of businesses to be licensed. The cost is almost always very modest and the procedure is a simple one. Call your local city or county clerks office to obtain details on exactly what is required in your area.

Your Letterhead and Envelope

In doing business by mail, a major contact between you and potential buyers is your letterhead and envelope. Don't skimp here. You don't have to spend a fortune, but you should make a nice business presentation. Nicely printed stationery will achieve this objective. While many "save" a few dollars by using a rubber stamp on envelopes and as substitute letterheads, I am convinced this is being penny wise and very dollar foolish. Your business stationery makes a statement about you and your business. Take the necessary steps to make it a positive statement.

Real Value—
The Key to Continued Success

Give your customer m-o-r-e than their money's worth

There is an old mail order axiom that goes something like this: "Put most of your money into your advertising and only a little into your product!" The theory is not without foundation. In many cases, mail customers have only your advertising as a criteria for placing their orders. Often they don't really know what to expect when their mailman delivers your package. This fact of mail selling has led many dealers to "promise the moon but only deliver a few specks of moon dust."

While I agree that much of your money must go into your sales vehicle (ads, circulars, brochures, catalogs or whatever), nevertheless, I urge you only to sell products you would be willing to order at prices you would be willing to pay. The real ripoff artists who promise a lot and deliver very little usually don't last long. Repeat business is a major factor in reaching mail order success, and nobody ever reorders from someone whom they feel cheated them. Then too, a guarantee of satisfaction is usually required to sell anything by mail. And if you guarantee satisfaction, and most mail customers expect a moneyback guarantee, you must refund returned merchandise or face trouble from the post office.

You will earn more money in the long run, and sleep better nights, by offering your mail order clients true value. Honesty may not always be the best policy, but it seems to be the only one that works!

Profit Ideas has gained positive national recognition with both book sellers and book buyers by producing the finest quality, in-demand, success, investment and business books. In the short run, we could save thousands of dollars in printing and production costs by cutting corners.

But over the long haul, our commitment to quality has dramatically expanded our business due to many re-orders from satisfied book buyers. This is how mail order fortunes are made!

A leading mail order operator, associated with "junk booklet publishing" (small reports of questionable value sold through ads that make wild, get-rich-quick claims) once remarked to me at a mail order trade show, "I don't know why Profit Ideas publishes such high quality paperback books. It's the ad or direct mail package that sells the publication. They don't even see it till they get it!"

After reminding him that he recently had complained to me and others that he was getting almost a 20% return factor (dissatisfied customers demanding a refund) and that his bounce-back sales (re-orders) were almost nil, I told him the truth about our book sales. The Profit Ideas return factor is less than 1% (the lowest in the industry), and my dealers earn substantial profits on both the front end (original orders) and the back end (repeat orders). Real value brings satisfaction. Customer satisfaction leads to repeat business. Repeat business builds mail order success!

It's difficult to build a solid mail order bookselling business on one-shot offers. Give them real value and they'll buy from you again and again. Also, having learned a valuable lesson years ago, I have given it this quotation: *Don't cheat or take advantage of your customer, you'll be the loser. Instead, win success by giving your customers their money's worth. And if you really want great success, **give your customers more than their money's worth.*** There are two great reasons why you should practice this principal. (1) It's the right thing to do. (2) It makes your customers happy. You can build a mega-profit mail order business with lots of happy customers.

A Business Checking Account

Once you establish your d.b.a. and secure a business license (if one is required in your locality), it's time to open your business checking account. In the mail order business you will soon be depositing a large number of checks and money orders. If there are several banks in your area, take some time to check them out individually. You are looking for one that charges the lowest service charges, charge per check written, etc. All banks are not the same. Comparison shopping could save you $100 or even more per year in banking fees.

You may also want to inquire about getting a credit card in your company name and/or attempt to secure a VISA/ Mastercard arrangement so that you can accept credit card purchases from your mail order book-buying customers. Often, a banker is somewhat reluctant to set you up with credit card privileges when you first start a new business. However, once your establish your company with the bank (6

Not all banks are the same. Give your business to the one who gives you the most value.

FREE
CHECKING
ACCOUNTS

FREE
PRINTED
CHECKS

INTEREST
PAID ON
CHECKING

to 12 months may be required to do this), they often become more cooperative.

You and the Law

Although there are very few rigid laws governing most types of mail order business, the ones in force should be adhered to. The primary laws you should be aware of are:

(1) All orders must be shipped within 30 days of receipt, or the customer made aware of the added anticipated delay, while being given the option to get his or her money back (*here at Profit Ideas it has always been our policy to ship our orders and our dealer dropship orders the same day they are received*).

(2) The product (or book) you send to your customer must be similar to that which was described in your ad or mailing circular.

(3) Unless you state that you offer no moneyback guarantee, you must return a customer's money if he or she returns the product in reasonably good shape. You can check with your local Better Business Bureau (BBB) and/or Chamber of Commerce concerning other laws.

WHY SELL "INFORMATION?"

Modern mail order, or direct response marketing, as it is now often called (hey, that's a mouthful!), is a multi-billion dollar business. In spite of severe recent postage increases, it continues to grow and prosper.

Almost anything can be sold by mail. For example, here is a partial list of products or services I personally have sold by mail, or have done the copywriting for the clients who sold them: Bibles, many types of books, candies, candles, catalogs, a cattle ranch, clocks, educational courses, diamonds (both real and simulated), dolls, lingerie, magazines, mailing lists, newsletters, opals and other gemstones, printing, radios, real estate, sunglasses, stud services for thoroughbred race horses, tapes, TVs and tape recorders, warehouse and office equipment, water purification systems, etc., etc., etc. How's that for diversification!

Although almost anything can and is sold by mail, some time ago I discovered the *almost perfect* product...

Once considered "a man's business," modern mail order selling is now very popular with enterprising women who want their fair share of the huge profits available.

INFORMATION!

Information—good information—is always sought after. It always sells! Today, more than ever before, people want advice and facts on almost every conceivable subject, from money-making to lovemaking, and from Astrology to Zoology, up-to-date information is a commodity in great demand. You can make extra bucks or mega-bucks, providing simple, but valuable information to millions of potential mail order buyers.

Selling information (books, manuals, reports, tapes, etc.) has so many advantages over most other types of products you could sell by mail. Over twenty years ago I started a spare-time mail order business. My initial products were novelties and gift items that I purchased wholesale from various U.S. manufacturers and distributors. I soon realized I needed more unusual products that also offered bigger profit margins. This led me to get involved in foreign trade. In the beginning that was very exciting. I imported lovely clocks from Germany, sunglasses from Taiwan and Korea, and radios and cassette tape players from Hong Kong and Japan. I sold these and other items retail in newspaper and magazine display ads, and wholesale to various American catalog dealers. Business was pretty good for a while and I was making some money, but there were some problems, too. I became concerned about slow shipping. An order sent to Hong Kong could take up to four months to arrive. I also was concerned about the significant number of items damaged in shipment. (The companies were pretty good about replacing damaged items, but this meant waiting additional weeks/months to receive replacements.)

I was longing for a new line of easy-to-get, unbreakable products to sell. Lucky for me, a friend of mine who was a writer suggested I write a book on importing and foreign trade, the profits available, pitfalls to avoid, and some sources of low-cost supply. Could I write a book?

My friend convinced me I could if I really wanted to. I

decided it was a darn good idea. I did it! My first book was quite small in size, and certainly no literary masterpiece. It was, however, easy to read and contained the magic ingredient—*valuable information!*

A few weeks after placing some ads, orders started to come in at a growing pace. I had a little winner on my hands. Best of all, I had discovered a "product" that was:

1. Easy to produce or purchase (wholesale or dropship) from others
2. Easy to sell
3. Easy to store
4. Easy to ship
5. Hard (almost impossible!) to "break"

Lord love a duck! I was excited! I contacted four or five different publishing sources, and soon had my own little 8-page catalog of business books and booklets. In addition to my own book, I featured about two dozen other titles. Although I didn't get rich overnight, it wasn't long before I was raking in some real money. Soon I was able to quit my "regular" job (which I disliked) and go full-time into a field I loved then, and love now—mail order book and information selling!

Take it from me—a guy who has been involved in the exciting, wild, sometimes confusing, wonderful world of mail order selling. Information packaged in the form of books, manuals, newsletters, tapes, etc., is the ideal mail order product.

This business is creative, challenging, fun, and it can be very, very profitable.

SELF-PUBLISHING

To enter the lucrative mail order information and book-selling business, you have three options:

(1) self-publish your own books or other materials
(2) sell items already published
(3) do both of the above.

Let me give you, first, the basics of self-publishing.

While the vast majority (probably 90%) of small publishers and self-publishers lose much or all of their money in their self-publishing efforts, there have been and will continue to be remarkable success stories.

Don't be discouraged when I mention that, perhaps, 90% of all self-publishers fail. It simply means that the vast majority who decide to enter this fascinating—but little understood—field do not prepare for success. Writing that book or report is only step one on the long ladder that leads to success. The desire to market aggressively and the ability to market

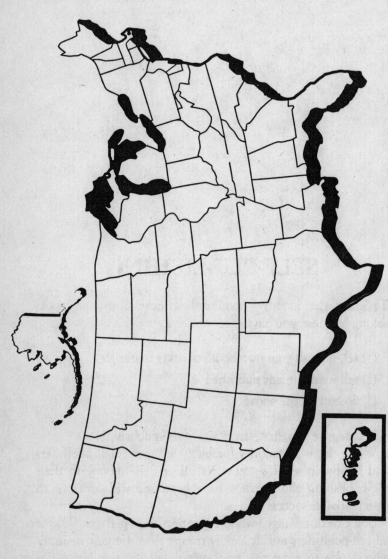

Selling information by mail lets you do business from anywhere in America, selling nationwide and worldwide.

selectively is the major factor that separates the winners from the losers. Don't write a book unless you are prepared to market it for all your worth! Most "literary types" fare much worse than non-literary entrepreneur types. A true-blue entrepreneur may not be a "born writer," but he or she is ready to learn, anxious to earn, and eager to sell. All ingredients that brew success!

You don't have to be a "gifted" writer to make big money with information.

This manual is written for anyone who would like to earn money—a little extra dough, or whole bunches of long green.

Ernest Hemingway, John Steinbeck, James Jones, Taylor Caldwell, William Shakespeare and Mickey Spillane (a boyhood favorite of mine), are *writers*. I'm just a pencil-pushing word seller, but I'm making nice money and enjoying myself. And you can, too.

I have prospered by writing and/or "packaging" well over three dozen books and manuals, but only one of them, to date, *How to Achieve Total Success*, qualifies as a work of art. Through a constant process of daily meditation and the practice of advanced *Mind Science* principles, I believe I was inspired during the six month period in which I wrote that book. I'm very proud of *Total Success*, and the positive effect it has had and continues to have, on lives all over the world. I'm also pleased with the success and profits generated from dozens of other practical business and investment works that I have produced in something less than an "inspired" state of mind and being. When it comes to either writing or marketing books, preparation is often more important than inspiration.

There is power in taking action. Although I believe in the benefits of meditation, I think most of us need to spend only 5% of our time thinking, planning and meditating, and 95% of our time taking positive action!

If you have decided to write and package some valuable information—stop thinking about it, stop talking about it—DO IT!

Don't let the "experts" trick you into thinking that you need an impressive training period and many years of formal education to write for pay. That's pure *horse manure!*

A positive mental attitude and an unyielding desire to succeed and "see it in print"—plus a willingness to share useful information can make you a winner in word-selling, information by mail business.

I offer no miracles, but in this manual you will find the techniques, tactics, concepts, guidelines and methods that can point you to success in writing and/or self-publishing. And that's all you need to enter and prosper in this fascinating arena.

ALWAYS GIVE THANKS FOR ALL THAT YOU ARE, ALL THAT YOU ARE NOT, AND ALL THAT YOU ARE BECOMING.

I've written dozens of books, hundreds of ads, countless magazine articles, and more. With the possible exception of Tyler G. Hicks and Herman Holtz, two very prominent business authors, I may well be today's most prolific money-making writer and author. I'm widely recognized as a leading expert on small business and home business opportunities, throughout the free world. Hey, that's good for my ego. I like it! However, by all odds, Russ von Hoelscher should never have been a leading expert at anything, much less a best-selling author. But you see, I always had some faith in God, and a little bit in me. I also was blessed to have some relatives and friends who believed in me. I learned early in life that thinking is fine, but unless you get involved in the *doing*, you can't make your dreams come true.

My advice to you: *If you believe in yourself and your project—DO IT!*

Profit Ideas began nine years ago as a very small press operation, and today is perhaps the fastest-growing entrepreneur publishing firm in America. Other recent self-publishing heroes who have gone on to win both fame and fortune include: Joe Karbo, Robert Shindler, Jerry Buchanan, Tyler Hicks, Dax, Robert Ringer, Dan Poynter, Dr. Wayne Dyer, Ben Suarez, Douglas Holmes, David Bendah, Bud Weckesser, Mark Haroldsen, John Wright, Sam Pitts, and Dr. Jeffrey Lant. And there are many, many others, many of whom I'm proud to call friends.

All of the above *self-publishing stars* as well as 90% of the successful self-published books in recent years are on business, investment, motivation and some form of moneymaking topics. In fact, it is my opinion that if you intend to get into publishing today, you better be selling vital information in the area of moneymaking, diet, health, religion, metaphysics/spirituality, gambling or sex. Fiction, poetry and general non-fiction almost always loses money for the small self-publisher.

With the exception of specialized information in the form of guidebooks or directories aimed at select markets (specific professionals, special industries, etc.), I would caution anyone against publishing any book outside of the subject matter just mentioned. The risk factor in any publishing venture is extremely high. With fiction, poetry, etc., the odds are overwhelmingly against you.

Stick to the basics (wealth-health-happiness) and you've got your best shot at success.

Below is my "people are interested in" chart. Every interest presented here is in some way related to the big 3: wealth, health and happiness.

Here is a partial list of what interests readers (information buyers):

PEOPLE'S INTERESTS

People Want To Be:

Loved
Appreciated
Admired
Beautiful
Creative
Powerful
Respected
Productive
Informed
Free
Successful
Recognized
Forgiven

People Want To Obtain:

More money
Advancement in business
Security for the future
More leisure time
Improved health
Self-esteem
Peace of mind
Self-control
Pleasure
Improved physical
    appearance
More personal prestige
Positive image

People Want To Do:

Their own thing
Start their own business
Express their individuality
Accomplish something
    important
Obtain affection & love
Important tasks
Improve themselves
Travel to exciting places
Have more fun
Do less work
Make a greater
    contribution

Almost everyone wants to "write a book," and almost anyone could. Most people have the ability, some have the drive, but few have the determination, organization and persistence. Therefore, the greatest need is for a simple "road map." The basic organizational plan will not only provide direction, it will promote drive and expose ability you may not have known you possessed. *We are all smarter and better than we think we are.* We just must learn how to get out of our own way!

Writing a simple report is easy, and writing a full-length book is not very difficult. *If you can think it and say it, you can write it!*

The secret is to take the "whole project" and break it down into little "pieces."

I can't teach you how to write brilliant poetry or fiction, but since it's a very hard sell anyway, don't worry about it. If you want to write fiction or poems, do it as your hobby. That way, if you ever sell it to a major publisher, it's a big bonus. If you don't, you at least have the satisfaction of doing something for yourself.

I want you to know about nonfiction. That's what is most likely to sell today. Nonfiction doesn't require any unique literary style, it is simply the packaging and sale of well-researched, organized, up-to-date information.

People want to know "how-to" and they will pay well to find out how. The information industry, the production and distribution of ideas and information as opposed to goods and services, now amounts to over 55% of our gross national product. There is money in information. To see how this market is being tapped by books, check the best seller lists in the back of *Publishers Weekly*, noting especially the "Trade Paperback" section. You'll be amazed at how many "how-to" titles make the best-seller lists.

Your best sources for this saleable information are from your own experience, plus research. Write what you know well and/or like best. Knowing a subject and/or liking a subject well enough to do necessary research will make the job of writing about it so much easier.

A Step-by-Step Guide
to Preparing Your Manuscript

Preparation of a saleable "how to" information book, report or manual, or a directory of valuable information—addresses, etc.—need not be considered a monumental task. By dividing the components of a self-publishing project into a compiled order, you'll discover that a book or directory is put together one piece at a time.

A directory is usually the easiest project to undertake, once the information or addresses have been compiled. For example: if you decided to publish a directory of Hong Kong suppliers of merchandise of interest to American importers, you might invest considerable time and effort to research and obtain hundreds of names of Hong Kong manufacturers and distributors of various merchandise. However, once this information has been obtained, arranging your information into classifications and then having it typeset (or just neatly typed), and prepared for printing in a directory format, would be quite easy and require little imagination.

Preparing a how-to book or manual is a little different. Let's take my recent home business book, *Stay Home and Make Money* as an example. Since this is a full-scale book, it presents us with more of a challenge than a short report or a compiled directory.

R & D (Research and Development): This is where we play Sherlock Holmes. Pertinent data is collected. We read and make notes. All serious **R & D** work begins at a good public library. Ask the librarian for *Bowker's Books in Print*, and lists of magazine articles on almost every conceivable subject. Other good sources for information on a wide range of topics include the U.S. government. Write for the current catalog of "Select U.S. Government Publications (Superintendent of Documents, United States General Post Office, Box 1821,

Washington, DC 20402). A Saturday afternoon can be well spent in one or more large used bookstores (found in all large cities and many small ones). There are great research treasures to be found in a used bookstore.

Although I use personal experiences (mine and those of others I know) in all of my books, for my home business book, *Stay Home and Make Money*, I did do a good bit of **R & D** (reviewing books, journals, and magazine articles) to uncover additional unusual and profitable home businesses to add to that book.

Select Your Chapters/Headings

By dividing your subject matter into chapter titles or headings, you cut a full-blown writing project down to manageable size. Here is how I did it for my *Stay Home and Make Money Book*.

I developed five major chapter (or section) headings to help me cut this project down to workable size.

1. How to Establish a Home Business that is Right for You.

2. Home Business Opportunities

3. Writing and Publishing Opportunities

4. How to Make Big Money in Mail Order

5. Supply Source Directory

With these five major sections for my book, each with its own file folder, it was easy for me to place material I produced or gathered from other sources, into the correct file folder.

Now, when I had some information on supplies and equipment needed to operate almost any home business, I knew where to put it—in the first section on establishing a home business.

When I had a hot business opportunity I knew I wanted in

my book—it was put in Section Two—Home Business Opportunities file. A source for low-cost printing? Sure! That goes in Section Five—the Source Directory, etc. Are you getting the picture? A big job is being broken down into easy-to-handle, smaller components.

Now, once the file folders are bulging full of assembled random notes, magazine clippings, my long-hand legal pad scribbling, etc., I can select one file folder at a time, and put things in more or less logical order, adding and/or deleting information, rearranging, etc. Once this is done, the writing and rewriting process begins.

By no means should you feel compelled to write your book page by page, chapter by chapter. Start anywhere you wish. Often it's a splendid idea to start with the chapter that interests you the most. Do anything you can to make your project a little joyful, instead of a Herculean ordeal.

When first you throw everything into some order you are working with what is called a "rough draft." Your manuscript is now definitely taking shape, but it's still "rough" and needs more work.

Editing: When the first draft is finished, regardless of how rough and unconcise it may appear, it's time to add, delete and hone your manuscript through the editing process. If you're not really a star editor type, and most of us aren't, hire someone who is. A journalism major at a local college is always eager to make some extra money. For a very reasonable fee—use $1.00 per page as a guide—he or she can help whip your manuscript into shape.

Ghost Writers: If you need lots of help to bring your book idea from conception to saleable (printed) state, you could hire a ghost writer to handle the entire project for you, or you could hire another writer to work side by side with you in the role of ghost co-writer and editorial assistant. Again, the cost for writing or editorial help is probably a lot less than you think. Good writers and editors come pretty cheap (except those with established "names"). I'm thankful I woke up years ago and realized that *the money is in the marketing* *and selling of books and information, not merely in writing and editing.* I recommend that you pay a flat fee for these services, and do not offer a royalty payment contract that will have these people sharing in book sale profits. Writing a book is hard work and takes some talent and determination. Selling a book at a profit takes a Master Marketing Genius. If you share profits with anyone, share with the man or woman who can successfully market!

Writing Style: Use the K.I.S.S. (Keep it Simple, Stupid) approach. Don't try to impress your readers with ten-dollar words. Use the 10¢ words they understand (obviously, you may include professional jargon if your information package is targeted at scientists, doctors, lawyers, etc.). Short sentences and short paragraphs. Everything must flow, and be clear and concise. If it's easy to read and informs, you have done your job well.

Protect Your Property
With a Copyright

Whatever you create on paper, be it a two-page "report" or a 2,000-page literary masterpiece, it is wise to protect your creative labor via the copyright method. This procedure is also simple and easy to obtain.

In 1976, after decades of confusion, the United States Congress updated copyright laws in this nation. Many new provisions were added, giving expanded protection to copyright holders.

Following is a brief, but hopefully, concise review of the new copyright law, plus information on how you can secure a copyright for everything you write.

What is a Copyright?

A copyright simply gives you the right to copy, distribute and sell an original work of authorship. It is a law protecting ownership. Generally, a person owns what he or she creates until he sells it, or assigns it to someone else, or until he or she accepts a salary for creating it (publishers hold the copyright on books that they publish). As a self-publisher (you as both publisher and author), you will secure your own copyright.

What we call copyright protection is the legal registration of that ownership. The copyright office, for a fee of $10, keeps a record of the date a property existed, to whom it belongs, and has on file in the Library of Congress two copies of the work. In cases of infringement litigation, these data are legal evidences that entitle the owner to obtain redress and collect damages. Copyright protection extends only to *works*; it does *not* extend to any idea, procedure, process, system, etc., regardless of the form in which it is described. That is, you can copyright sequences of words or sounds, of which a copy exists. You copyright the copy, not the content.

A person owns this right to copy only for a specific time. For works created after January 1, 1978, the new law provides a term lasting for the author's life, plus an additional 50 years after the author's death. For works made for hire, and for anonymous and pseudonymous works (unless the author's identity is revealed in Copyright Office records), the new terms will be 75 years from publication or 100 years from creation, whichever is shorter.

Under the old law, the term of copyright was 28 years, plus a second renewal term of 28 years, or 56 years in all. Under the new law, works in their first term must still be renewed, but they can be renewed for a term of 47 years, making a total of 75 years. Copyrights already in their second term at the time the new law went into effect are automatically extended up to the maximum of 75 years without the need for further renewal.

Step by Step
Copyright Guide

To secure a copyright for a non-dramatic work, here are the three steps you must take:

First: Publish the work *with the copyright notice*. The law requires that a copyright notice in a specified form "shall be placed on all publicly distributed copies" of the work, on the title page, or (more commonly) on the back side of the title page, or as part of the colophon in a magazine. Use of the copyright notice consists of three elements: (1) the symbol "©", or the word "Copyright," or the abbreviation "Copr."; (2) the year of the first publication; and (3) the name of the copyright owner. For example: "Copyright 1987, Profit Ideas." (Copyrights can be a person's name or a company's name.)

Unlike the old law, the new law provides procedures for correcting errors in the copyright notice, and even for curing the omission of the notice altogether. However, failure to comply with the requirement for copyright notice correctly may result in loss of some areas of valuable copyright protection. If not corrected within five years, you can blow your entire copyright.

Second: Fill out the proper application forms. For a non-dramatic literary work, the proper form would be Form TX. Write the Copyright Office for the blanks, then fill them out carefully, using a typewriter or dark ink, after reading the instructions.

Third: Send the required fee, the required copies, and the completed application to "The Registrar of Copyrights, Library of Congress, Washington, D.C. 20559." The fee for a first copyright of a book is now $10, which must be paid by check or money order, made payable to "The Registrar of Copyrights." You are required to deposit two copies of the published work with the Library of Congress (one copy of unpublished works). These are the copies that become evidence in infringement litigation. Send the fee, the copies, and the application together.

When the Registrar of Copyrights has processed your application and filed the copies, you will receive an official certificate of copyright, bearing the official seal of the Copyright Office. That certificate is your evidence of ownership.

Surprising as it may seem, many self-publishers never bother to copyright their work. This is often the case with publishers of small booklets, reports, etc., while some new self-publishers seem to worry too much about someone "stealing" their precious literary creations. Others seem to worry, not at all, and don't ever bother to protect, in any way, what they write.

While it's unlikely another publisher will knock off your information book, manual, etc., word for word, and too there is little you can do about them stealing your ideas or concepts, it's still a good idea to copyright everything you write and publish.

How Much $ is Needed?

If you intend to self-publish your own book (or one written by someone else for you), you must bear all expenses. While it is hard to put an actual dollar figure on a self-publishing effort which would include prep, printing, promotion, advertising, distribution, etc., one of the factors to be considered would be whether or not your book is to be a big hardcover, a perfect-bound paperback, or a smaller book or booklet? How many pages, illustrations, etc., plus how extensive will your promotion/advertising campaign be? Overall, I think the average self-publisher is making a $5,000 to $15,000 commitment to publish and promote a book today. However, the range can be anywhere from a few thousand dollars to a whopping one hundred thousand bucks!

There is good news and bad news concerning self-publishing. The good news first: you maintain total control over your book. It will rise or fall based upon its content and your overall promotional/marketing efforts. The bad news is that the process is expensive and time consuming. Also, the vast majority of self-published works lose money.

Contrary to popular belief, writing a book is only a job 10 to 20% complete. There is great joy in seeing your literary labors born through the printing process. However, unless you can **crack the marketing rock**, your publishing venture is doomed to failure.

A lack of forceful and creative sales promotion and distribution efforts can turn even a good book into a financial dud. I've seen too many "good books" fail for lack of strong marketing, while watching some "bad books" become winners.

You gotta *tell 'em to sell 'em*, and that means hustle and bustle in the arena of sales, marketing and promotion.

While it's not that difficult now for anyone with some money to self-publish their own works, the novice publisher will soon discover publication is only the first step on the ladder of success in self-publishing. It is the vital areas of distribution and marketing that will decide ultimate victory or defeat of any publishing venture.

Too often writers/publishers order 5,000 or more books, manuals or booklets printed, and then ask themselves, "How am I going to get them distributed and sold?" Friends and relatives are only going to put a very small dent in a 5,000 book run, unless the author is immensely popular and has a huge circle of friends or fans. Successful distribution strategy begins prior to publication, not as an afterthought while staring at many boxes of your books stacked high in your garage or spare bedroom.

Sell Those Books!

Here are just some of the proven ways to sell books (many of them very innovative):

- Sell through other book distributors
- Sell direct to bookstores
- Sell to libraries and schools
- Sell via telephone solicitation
- Sell via mail order space ads
- Sell via direct mail
- Sell through radio and TV commercials
- Sell at swap meets and flea markets
- Sell door to door
- Sell at local parks and recreation areas
- Sell by handing out ad flyers at concerts, churches, conventions, universities, etc.

Every one of the abovementioned techniques of selling self-published books has been used successfully to market the written word. At first glance, a few of these methods may seem very unusual, but they have worked for others—why not for you? If you abhor lots of personal contact with potential book buyers, some of the above distribution techniques will not be your cup of tea. You'll have to try more conventional sales tactics (working with distributors, retailers, selling by mail, etc.). However, if you don't mind "getting involved" with people to sell your books, your means of distribution can cover the gamut of distribution methods.

The real secret of successful book distribution is to EXPAND YOUR THINKING. "Think Sales!!"

Successful mail order information-selling is the chief topic of this book, but I do want you aware of the many alternative methods for selling any books or other materials you self-publish, or obtain for resale from another publisher.

Get busy telling people about the merits of your books.

"THE MORE YOU TELL, THE MORE YOU SELL." Remember William H. Johnsen's ten important two-letter words: *"IF IT IS TO BE, IT IS UP TO ME!"*

NOTE: Anyone who is planning to self-publish needs a strong support network, beginning with an excellent book printer who can deliver good workmanship at reasonable prices. An extensive source directory in the back of this book will help the new self-publisher save time, hassle and money on production, marketing, etc.

You can start your business in your spare hours, day or night,
without leaving your job (at least not just yet).

ESTABLISHING YOUR OWN PROFITABLE BOOK DISTRIBUTORSHIP

While some will enter the book business by self-publishing their own books, an easier, safer and much less expensive method is now available. I'm ready, willing and very able to help you become a successful distributor of an extremely fast-selling lineup of desirable books and tapes.

It's only fair I now remind you that I am the director of the Profit Ideas Fast Start Distributor Program, and that we offer the undisputed No. 1 mail order book distributorship in the land. If you *believe* I am merely blowing smoke or tooting my own whistle, I urge you to compare the quality of the impressive lineup of Profit Ideas books with all the booklets, bulletins, folios, reports, etc., that are so commonly (and often so worthlessly) offered as "books" from so many mail order publishers. We have the best program, because we have the best books! *And you get me at no extra charge!*

My commitment to excellence in living, loving and

achieving has been truly complemented by the commitment to value that goes into the production and marketing of the Profit Ideas books. We may spend three, four, or even five times more money in production/printing costs for a book than several of the "junk booklet" publishers are willing to spend, but the bottom line is that we eventually make more money and so do our distributors.

Our commitment to quality pays off. Someone may be able to staple together a few printed sheets, call it a book and sell it for ten, fifteen or even twenty dollars, to the unsuspecting. But will these people ever send that dealer another order? Not very likely. I am appalled by all the questionable materials being sold from ads or by direct mail today. Profit Ideas periodically orders books and booklets from others, just to keep updated on what the competition is up to, and with only a few exceptions, I am shocked and dismayed with what so many are peddling—one-page "reports" for five dollars or more, 5 or 10 page booklets for $10 and up, etc. And that's not the worst of it. The really sad thing is the content of these reports, booklets, etc., is often so poorly written and contains unrealistic and unproven moneymaking advice.

THE "FAST START"
BOOK PROGRAM

After 20 years of day-by-day involvement in the mail order and book-selling business (I've sold books by mail for 20 years. Also, I have written, published, distributed books and owned 9 retail bookshops), I decided, in cooperation with publisher George Sterne and Profit Ideas, to make available a totally new business opportunity to people interested in starting a new business of their own. No pie-in-the-sky, get-rich-overnight scheme, but a very lucrative and exciting business opportunity that can be started with very little investment part-time and then built into a very substantial moneymaker.

The mail order book business is a multi-billion-dollar business and I feel this program is the only one of its kind.

I realize there are a few other distributors or publishers who do sell mail order book dealerships or "reprint rights" (often at outrageous fees!), but have you ever seen the "books" available from some of these sources? Often they are sloppy-looking bulletins, booklets or reports—not really books in the true sense. Much worse, the information they peddle is so often outdated, unproven and/or so poorly written. It really makes me sad to see people wasting their money trying to sell or use such trash.

To win success and then remain successful in the mail order book business, you must build your business on rock, not quicksand. *Every book published by PROFIT IDEAS offers uncompromising value. These are big, beautiful, quality books. Most importantly, between the covers you'll find the ultimate in new profit strategies and wealth-building knowledge.* We now make available to you these quality books and the best distribution program ever conceived. I will not only give you this great business opportunity, *I will stand by you and keep you on the road to ever-increasing profits. To accomplish this goal, I offer my "FAST START" dealers my free consultation, any time (during business hours) you require it. I believe one helps himself the most by helping others.*

Some Questions and Answers
Re: the "FAST START" Program

Q: What type of books do you offer?

A: The PROFIT IDEAS books are all quality business, home business, mail order, and success titles. They are all proven fast-sellers. Each book is in an attractive format and is a full-sized book, loaded with good information which has wide appeal.

Q: How much money can I make as a "FAST START" PROFIT IDEAS book distributor?

A: You will make $6.50 or more for each sale you make when we dropship. That's $650 for 100 books, $6,500 for 1,000 books, $65,000 for 10,000 books, etc. Actually, you could make much more since you will be able to "group sell" books, offering six different books for the price of five, thus making $32.50 each time you sell these and other special deals. And if you buy in quantity, your profits will be even more substantial than if we dropship for you. Also, our new cassette tape programs allow you to make up to $100 and more, per sale.

Q: *Do I have to stockpile books?*

A: Absolutely not. Profit Ideas does all this for you. You do not have to carry any stock unless you want to. Using our dropship method, you keep 50% of all money received, and we do the stocking and shipping. We will send all orders directly to you as required by you, or if you prefer, we will dropship your order directly to your customer. If we ship to your customer, we suggest that you send us your shipping label made out to your customer so that he or she is aware only of doing business with you. All easy ordering instructions, how you never have to purchase anything from us until you have been paid for it, etc., will all be included in your "FAST START DISTRIBUTORS KIT." You will know, step by step, exactly how to make big money in this super business.

Q: *Why appoint distributors? Why not do all your own selling and keep all the money?*

A: Ray Kroc, the founder of McDonald's once said, "I started my hamburger chain with one location; now there are over 10,000. If it wasn't for our franchise owner-operators, I could not keep on top of this business!" It is estimated that there are over thirty-five million potential customers for business, success and money-making books. Too many for one company to hope to effectively reach. PROFIT IDEAS is willing to share our success with you and a limited number of others. And you can start from scratch. We charge no franchise fees and have no "extra charges," etc. You work only when you want to. Of course, a little effort on your part will be required if you wish to build a super successful book-selling business. Yours truly, Russ von Hoelscher, will show you the way, but you must be willing to put in a few, pleasurable hours per week to get things rolling.

Q: *Isn't there a danger that you will soon have too many distributors?*

A: Absolutely not! Once I have 100 active, producing, money-making Fast Start distributors, no other distributors will be accepted. Trouble is, many of my would-be distributors order the big kit, and then use the money-making plans in these super books to carve out their fortunes, without ever getting involved in the sale and distribution of our books and tapes. *Hark onto me: use our books to make money for yourself, but also make big money selling them to others.* The Fast Start distributors program is a winner! I don't mind the fact that many are ordering the big kit just to get six of our fabulous books at a big discount, but you should really consider the tremendous moneymaking opportunity in selling these books and tapes to others.

Q. *When does my free consultation service start?*

A: Your free consultation service begins just as soon as you send for your "FAST START DISTRIBUTORS KIT." My direct line phone number will be included in your dealership package. Of course, you may write anytime. When you write, please give your phone number as I may want to call you immediately.

Q: *To be able to sell books, will I be supplied with brochures, flyers, etc., from you or will I print my own from camera-ready copy you provide?*

A: The choice is yours. Flyers will be available from us at our cost or you can receive camera-ready work—at no cost—from us and have a local print shop run off as many as you need. If you wish to use our series of beautiful 2-sided, 4-color flyers (see the one enclosed in this mailing), it will be less expensive to order them through us. Since we print these hundreds of thousands at a time, you will be able to get them from us at our cost: as little as 2½¢ each. These color flyers really pull in the orders and only need a simple order form with your name and address to get the business! Ready to use ads, sources of supplies, including where to get effective mailing lists, everything is included in your kit.

Q: Is this really a limited offer?

A: Absolutely! We are after quality, not quantity. A great part-time or full-time opportunity is not only knocking on your door, it's pounding!!! Send for your kit today. Let it be your blueprint to mail order mega-bucks!

Q: In the future, will other books be available in addition to the six I receive with my "Fast Start Distributor's Kit"?

A: Yes. We already have other books and manuals available, plus new, exciting cassette tape programs, etc., and when you become a Profit Ideas independent distributor, you offer only quality merchandise that people are eager to buy. You can't miss if you'll work with this program, provided that you are sincere and follow proven, easy guidelines. Don't miss this remarkable opportunity. Send for your "Kit" today. See Page 120 for details.

What Others are Saying About These Books and My Program

Just a few of the many, many testimonials we continually receive concerning our books and tapes:

"In an age of many misrepresentations and questionable consumer advertising, I am pleased that Russ von Hoelscher makes no compromises. I find his business, moneymaking and investment

writing to be first-class and extremely helpful."

W.H. Andrus
Attorney-at-Law, NY

*"Congratulations! **How to Achieve Total Success** is interesting, innovative and helpful."*

Norman Vincent Peale
World-famous author,
lecturer, clergyman

*"I've passed a resolution to name a day to honor **"Total Success"** and Russ von Hoelscher. This book is truly a great, great achievement."*

Mayor Steve Lockman
Lancaster, MN

"...Russ von Hoelscher can help anyone find success and themselves..."

THE DAILY CALIFORNIAN

"Magnificent and very motivational..."

Howard Jan, author of
THE SUCCESS JOURNAL

*"From deep depression after the loss of my job and a divorce, and with serious thoughts of committing suicide, to success, money and love, sweet love! I thank God for what **How to Achieve Total Success** has done for me.*

Name withheld
by request
Boca Raton, FL

*"**Total Success** and **"Secrets of the Millionaires"** have changed my life. More money, satisfaction, power and happiness are now mine! Thanks a million, Russ and George."*

Cal Kern
Houston, TX

"Secrets of the Millionaires" teaches how you can become a millionaire—there is no reason why you can't strike it rich!"

GLOBE
(weekly news magazine)

"I answer a lot of ads for get-rich books and plans. Usually I'm disappointed in what I receive. But your books and tapes are fantastic, even better than you say they are."

A. Scott
Brantford, Ont.
Canada

"Stay Home and Make Money" is the very best book on the subject of making money at home, starting from scratch."

HBO MAGAZINE

"Russ von Hoelscher's books, cassette tapes, and wealth-building program have set a new, high standard for our industry."

Al Galasso
BOOKDEALERS WORLD

"I recommend all of Russ von Hoelscher's fine success and money-making books and tapes."

Melvin Powers
(famous author/publisher and
owner of Wilshire Book Co.)

"These are marvelous books and cassette tapes."

Dottie Walters
(author and famous
professional speaker)

"How You Can Make a Fortune Selling Information by Mail" is vital to any entrepreneur who wants to make big money by packaging information and selling it through ads or direct mailing. Mr. Hoelscher, a leader in this field, gives you valuable

inside information."

"This treasury of home business opportunities offers potential entrepreneurs dozens of hot business ideas, all of which can be started from home during spare time."

"Selling dust from your vacuum cleaner (honest!) is just one of the hundreds of ways to make extra money (in this book)—this book is H-O-T—HOT!" *(Stay Home and Make Money)*

"The very best of the new crop of start your own business books—these big books not only tell you what you must do to go into business, but also help you pick the right opportunity for you."

"...Complete step-by-step information on how to establish and operate a lucrative small business of your own...teaches how to make money in huge chunks!"

"Opportunity is knocking! I know this business is a true gold mine because I've made my own fortune selling information by mail. Congratulations, Russ, for helping others achieve true financial freedom!"

"The best money-making books today are written by Russ von Hoelscher, and his "Fast Start" program is first class.

"Russ von Hoelscher is America's No. 1 teacher of money-making strategies. The new FAST START program is the only book dealership that offers superior quality books and audio cassette tapes, plus personal phone consultation with expert marketing advice."

Independent Entrepreneur

Now that you know how strongly I believe in the *"FAST START"* program, let's get into the *nuts and bolts* of selling books by mail.

If you have further questions regarding this special book dealership program, please call me at:

(619) 432-6913

10 a.m. to 5 p.m.
Monday through Friday

or write:

RUSS VON HOELSCHER
Profit Ideas
254 E. Grand Ave.
Escondido, CA 92025

Several years ago I realized cassette tapes were rapidly becoming more popular. Profit Ideas now offers Fast Start dealers both books and tapes.

SUCCESSFUL MAIL ORDER ADVERTISING

When you have the right books and/or other "information products" to sell (yours, those of another reputable publisher, or a combination of both), you're ready to get serious about advertising and promotion.

Print advertising comes in two major forms: display (space) ads, or classified ads. However, there is another important form of advertising (promotion) which is called publicity.

I'm all in favor of obtaining all the publicity possible, since this really means free advertising in an editorial context. However, any publicity you can get should be considered icing on the cake. It usually takes paid advertising to build your book/information business. Publicity should be considered an added bonus that can get you off to a fast start.

How to Obtain Free Publicity

Free editorials and "product news" information is offered by consumer and trade publications with "shopping" sections, or product information sections. The editors of these publications are willing to offer timely write-ups on products they feel will be of genuine interest to their readers.

You solicit editorial mentions by sending a news release plus a sample of your product with a clear 3x4 or 4x5 photograph of your product (if the product is quite expensive, you may wish to send only the photo and release).

The news release should be in double-spaced format. It should give a brief description of your product—service or new book—its benefits (for editorial purposes, editors want factual information, not glowing ad copy hype).

Since these free write-ups can be an excellent source of thousands of dollars of free advertising and publicity, you may wish to consider having a professional prepare your releases. The stakes here are high. A few positive mentions in national publications can generate a harvest of orders.

It is vital that you do not waste your time, effort and samples to the wrong media. If your product is aimed at opportunity seekers, don't bother requesting editorial mention in publications aimed at wine lovers. Some folks who are connoisseurs of fine vintage may also be seeking moneymaking information, but the media will not be right.

Editors offer write-ups on unique services and products that they think will interest a large section of their readership. Target marketing is the key to success.

Book Reviews

If you're selling books, booklets, manuals or printed or taped courses, in addition to going after general news release publicity you can also seek book reviews. The "book review" is an excellent source of unpaid advertising. This is the most effective and least expensive means of promoting your literary efforts.

Using Standard Rate and Data again as a source of potential media (and literally thousands of publications review books), you should easily find at least 200 or more publications as potential sources for your book reviews. If only 20% of these respond with a printed review, results could be very gratifying. Since editors are a busy lot, I strongly recommend you include your own "sample review." You may be surprised at how many will print it just as you submit it, especially if it is well-written and at least somewhat objective. Editors tend to be overworked, and sometimes like to receive a release that is *ready to print*.

Get all the free publicity you can, but also realize selective paid advertising is vital to your success.

Classified Advertising

Many mail order entrepreneurs make their mail order starts via classified advertising. Many operators have found success using this approach. Mail order beginners with limited advertising knowledge and/or limited cash are often best advised to "test the mail trade waters" in this medium.

A short (20 words or less), well-written classified is often the lowest cost effective method of advertising with the best overall dollar-for-dollar return.

Pinpoint the Media

As with display ads, you must be certain your classified ads are in the correct media. Start by searching for all available media "likely" to fit your specific offer.

Write for several sample copies to "likely" magazines and newspapers listed by Standard Rate and Data. This great media directory is available at most public libraries. However, classified ad information is not always mentioned. When you find a magazine that appears tailormade for advertising your product, write for rates.

Some magazines which do not have classifieds will accept small, ½" display ads. Other publications without classifieds do not accept any ad under the 1" size. If you're unfamiliar with the magazine, request a sample copy and rate card to find out.

Your ad budget may not expand beyond placing an ad in only half a dozen publications. Nevertheless, it is wise to select your classified ad media from as many publications as possible. Receiving free sample copies of hundreds of various newspapers and magazines is a bonus to operating your own mail sales business. There are a few publications which will only send you a rate card and no sample. Most will include a current or recent back issue in their media package. I, for one, would not advertise in any publications that I have never seen. I urge you to become familiar with any publication you intend to advertise in.

Sales or Inquiries?

I have found that well over 90% of the successful classified advertisers use "two-step" inquiry advertising. Making classifieds pay on the "order direct basis" is not very easy. Still, some dealers do make this method pay, but only if they are selling a small booklet or some other item priced under $5.00.

Information sellers of "booklets," "how-to plans," "sources of supply," "recipes," etc., often are able to get cash with order from a small classified ad. Those of us who sell full-size books and manuals must use the two-step, inquiry method.

Listed below are a few such cash-with-order ads that have been running for many months during the past year, leading me to believe they are working quite well for their operators.

Get Rich in mail order
selling simple information.
Free details. Name & address.

Success! Love! Money! Power! You
can have it all! Free details.
Name & address.

Stay Home and make money. Hundreds
of plans. Free information.
Name & address

"Secrets of the Millionaires"
revealed. Free details. Name & address.

You can achieve "Total Success"
using the Science Of Mind. Free
information. Name & address.

You will notice... all of these inquiry ads have one thing in common—they all use the magic word FREE! If you use your advertising to generate inquiries, always use this motivating four-letter word.

Some dealers, especially newcomers, offer free literature but request the reader to enclose a Self-Addressed Stamped Envelope (SASE) or a loose stamp to cover postage. This tactic will help you cut your postage bill. It also will greatly reduce the number of replies you receive. Overall, when advertising "free details," it is more profitable to keep it simple and keep it easy to reply. If you offer free information, let it be free!

Getting the Most for the Least Money Spent

Good classified ad writing is nothing more or less than good advertising copy in capsule format. While I would not suggest a beginner write his own large display ads, circulars, etc., most mail dealers, even beginners, can learn how to write a good classified ad of 20 words or less.

Since ad rates in national publications range anywhere from 75¢ to $10 per word for classified ads, you must use as few words as possible to convey your message.

But don't use this kind of a "few words that say little" approach:

Books for sale.
Free details.
Name & address.

The above ad saves some money on advertising cost by using very few words. It is also almost certainly doomed to failure, even if it pulls a large amount of inquiries. Since there are literally thousands of different ways to earn money, chances are remote that this "blind ad" will receive enough selective inquiries to make it pay off. When it comes to inquiry ads, it is how much net total income is earned from mailing your sales literature (after deducting all expenses) that determines whether you have a winner or not.

Now here is basically the same ad with just a few more words added:

New, profitable, start your own
business manuals, opportunity,
and home business books.
Free details. Name & address.

This ad will probably generate a better response, and every inquiry will know you're offering information relating to starting a business. Thus, you will be mailing your offer to people who have some idea as to what they are responding to. This type of responder is far more qualified than someone who answered a blind ad and has absolutely no idea as to what type of mail business you operate. The more qualified the responder (up to a certain point!), the better your chances to get the order.

Don't misunderstand me, it is important that there be some "mystery" in all your advertising. I believe in Elmer Wheeler's sales philosophy, "sell the sizzle, not the steak," and I also know mail order customers love to open letters and packages with some "surprise" in them. Thus, the sharp operator gives them a "hint" of what is offered but holds back enough to "whet their appetite." This should never be a problem with classified ads. Using only 20 words or less (the average classified ad is around 15 words), you can only offer a very brief description (taste) of what you're promoting.

The blind ad brings in the blind inquiry. Rarely will you see profits from this approach. Use punchy words, including the word FREE, and tell them a little about your books.

How to Write a Classified Ad
(Step-by-Step)

(A) Look over dozens of publications' classified sections to get a "feel" for classified ads. Pay particular attention to ads from other mail order booksellers.

(B) Take a large piece of paper and write down everything of interest you would list about the book or books you intend to sell.

(C) Determine and circle which words are the "key words," most likely to motivate the reader.

(D) Incorporate the five important elements of a good classified ad:

    (1) Gain the reader's attention.

    (2) Make your promise.

    (3) Tell what it is.

    (4) The price (or "free").

    (5) Your abbreviated address with "key code."

Here is an actual successful classified ad that incorporates all five important elements:

Make $2,000 weekly selling
information by mail. Free
details: Profit, 254-C
E. Grand Avenue
Escondido, CA 92025

The above 15-word ad, counting the zip code (some publications don't charge for the zip) employs all five elements. The "C" in 254-C E. Grand Avenue is the "key" for this particular ad. It is important to key all ads so you can determine which media works best for your offers.

Note: If you counted 16 words in the above ad, you have counted "San Diego" as two words. In fairness to advertisers in all cities—even a long one like San Juan Capistrano—most publishers now count any city name as only one word. That's just about the only "break" they give advertisers. Now most charge an additional word for your zip code.

Testing

Once you have a product and a market for a classified ad campaign, it is time to test. Since time is important in mail selling, you should arrange for quick testing, if possible. It can take up to three months to place advertising in monthly media. A long time to wait. You can cut this time in half or less by testing it in weekly publications.

The supermarket tabloids (*National Enquirer, Globe, The Star, National Examiner,* etc.,) offer excellent media for many books. *Grit* offers good general (rural-oriented) mail order media.

Your quest must always be to find those special (for you!) classified columns that will produce a ton of inquiries, followed by a high yield of actual orders.

While hunting for your rich mother lode advertising media, you should stick with any and all media that produce a profit, even a small profit. Nobody ever lost money in mail order making a profit.

As for how long to run classified ads in any media in which a test proves profitable, my standard advice is for as long as it shows a bottom line profit.

"Till forbid" is the term you can use to place ads in all media that tests indicate to be profitable. Placing individual insertion orders takes time, and you run the risk of missing publication deadlines. "Till forbid" simply means you are granting the publication the right to run your ad until such time as you forbid—cancel!

Classification is Important

In dealing with classified media, especially those with several pages of classifieds like the *National Enquirer*, it is important to be listed under the right "Classification."

Once you achieve some mail sales success, you may wish to test your ads under various classifications. Until then, play copycat! Place your ads under the same classifications as the competition. One notable caution: several mail order book sellers tend to gravitate to a classified heading that may read:

BOOKS, BOOKLETS, PAMPHLETS

Don't do it! For some weird reason, this classification is often the graveyard of booksellers, especially opportunity book sellers. If you're selling opportunity/business, such as the Profit Ideas titles, the two classifications that work best are:

MONEYMAKING OPPORTUNITIES
or
BUSINESS OPPORTUNITIES

The opportunity magazines (*Successful Opportunities, Money-Making Opportunities, Opportunity, Income Opportunities, Making Profits,* etc.) are good advertising media for money-making books.

Even faster testing can be done in daily newspapers. Just keep in mind that dailies go to everyone and anyone. It is a "shotgun approach" that won't work for every type of offer.

Key point: No medium will work for every type of offer. You must seek out the media whose general editorial, overall content and advertising thrust is best suited to the books you're selling.

Don't overspend testing any one publication. Rather than place multiple runs in only a few publications, it is usually best to run "one time tests" in several potentially good publications. Your key coding will then tell you which ones to reschedule in. Key all ads and keep good records of inquiries and sales.

Order Results— Not the Number of Inquiries— Determine Success

If you're selling payment with order, the response to your ad will make or break your offer. However, in the case of inquiry advertising, the bottom line is follow-up sales.

Anyone who has been active in running classified inquiry ads for any time knows that some publications pull many inquiries, but few convert to orders, while others pull several orders on smaller amounts of inquiries. The bottom line tells the tale.

Mailings and Follow-up

In using inquiry advertising, it is essential that you get your sales literature to your prospect while he or she is hot. Fast turn-around is most desirable. All inquiries should be processed quickly. If your two-step mail program is working smoothly, you will mail your offer to each prospect within 24 to 48 hours of receiving his inquiry.

How many times should you follow-up? This question can only be answered as it relates to your own singular proposition. You mail and remail as long as it is profitable to do so.

Only by testing will you be able to determine this. However, at least two follow-ups to your original mailing (spaced 10 to 15 days apart) should be made.

A company in Missouri that offers a home study correspondence course has found it profitable to make nine consecutive mailings (the original plus 8 follow-ups, spaced two weeks apart) to every single inquiry they receive. This is far more than the number used by most mail dealers. It does illustrate my point. Your own testing and records will tell you how many mailings you can afford to make to every inquiry you receive.

Four mailings (the original and 3 follow-ups) is just right for the Profit Ideas book mailings and most mail order book selling efforts.

Display Advertising

Much of what has already been said concerning classified advertising (defining a market that can be reached, selecting products to reach your market that are conducive to mail sales, testing, etc.) also applies to display advertising.

Preparing copy for display ads is usually best left to professional copywriters. It is not impossible for you to learn how to write result-getting space advertising, but it is certainly no job for the inexperienced. The money you save in not paying a good copywriter could be only a small part of the money wasted on advertising that falls flat.

RECORDS TELL YOU WHERE YOU'RE AT. Since the bottom line is all important, you must keep accurate records. On the following page is a monthly order/inquiry sheet printed here with permission from the excellent direct marketing book *Form Aides for Direct Response Marketing* ($14.95 postpaid, from: Publishers Media. Dept. DR, Box 546, El Cajon, CA 92022). Anyone doing any kind of business by mail will benefit by ordering a copy of this important manual.

Selecting Space Advertising

Placing large space (display) ads in major print media (magazines and newspapers) is probably the fastest way to make or lose money in mail order.

Selecting the right publication for your ad is no easy task. Even the professionally prepared ad copy (forgive my immodesty!) used to sell the Profit Ideas books must be carefully placed in the most likely publications. As an advertiser you must not only consider the circulation of a given publication, but also the demographics and psychographics of the publication's readership.

Display ads are sold by the "line" (most classified ad space is sold by the word). 14 "lines" make one inch of ad space (an average small one-inch ad is often approximately two inches wide by one inch deep). To sell books directly from the ad at prices of $10 or more, you almost always need a large

Ad Response Record

Publication_____ Issue_____ Page_____ Key_____
Proposition_____ Version_____
On sale date_____ Size_____ Position_____
Cost of ad_____ Circulation_____ CPM_____

	DATE	INQUIRIES		ORDERS		CASH SALES	
		Number Received	Total to date	Number Received	Total to date	Day's Sales	Total Sales
1							
2							
3							
4							
5							
6							
7							
8							
9							
10							
11							
12							
13							
14							
15							
16							
17							
18							
19							
20							
21							
22							
23							
24							
25							
26							
27							
28							

ad. If you're dealing with a magazine with standard 8½x11 pages, you'll need at least a one-half page ad, and a full page ad will usually pull best.

You can easily spend three thousand dollars or more to place a full page space ad in just one national publication. Space advertising is not cheap.

High cost per ad is one big disadvantage of running large display ads. The major positive factor is: if your display ad brings home lots of orders and earns you a profit, this method is the most simple method to run a money-making mail order book-selling business.

When it's working right, it's a jewel!

Some of the Best Publications

If you're selling books on success, business, money-making activities, etc., here is a partial list of publications for your consideration (all of these, quite naturally, accept display ads and most of them also accept classifieds):

DAILY NEWSPAPERS

Des Moines Register
Los Angeles Times
Los Angeles Herald-Examiner
Detroit Free Press
Philadelphia Enquirer
Rocky Mountain News
Chicago Tribune
Chicago Sun Times
Omaha World Herald
Cincinnati Post

Phoenix Republic Gazette
Portland Oregonian
Minneapolis Star
St. Paul Pioneer Press
Newark Star-Ledger
Baltimore Sun
Houston Chronicle
Dayton Spring News
St. Petersburg Times
Santa Ana Register

SUPERMARKET TABLOIDS

Globe
The Star

National Enquirer
National Examiner

GENERAL EDITORIAL/
MAIL ORDER SECTIONS

Grit

Cappers Weekly

Moneysworth

The Spotlight

SALES/OPPORTUNITY/BUSINESS

Get Rich News

Income Opportunities

Moneymaking Opportunities

Financial Opportunities

Spare-Time Opportunities

In Business

Success Opportunities

Wealth

Entrepreneur Advertiser

Entrepreneur

American Business

Venture

Selling Direct

Success

Successful Opportunities

Opportunity

SPORTS/CAMPING

Field and Stream

Outdoor Life

Camping Journal

Trailer Life

SCIENCE/MECHANICS/AUTO

Popular Science

Home Mechanic

Old Cars Weekly

Family Handyman

Car Craft

Popular Mechanics

SPECIAL INTEREST

Reason

Human Potential

Book Dealers World

Ebony

Fate

Home-Business News

L.A. Advertiser	Progressive Farmer
Mother Earth News	New Age
Family Travel Log	Holistic Life
Venture Capital News	Penny Stock Journal
Writers Digest	Firehouse
Soldier of Fortune	Treasure
Winning	Better Living

Two Major Mail Order Ad Agencies

The following two leading mail order advertising agencies can place ads for you in many different publications. You may wish to write them for free information on their services:

National Mail Order—P.O. Box 5, Sarasota, FL 33578

Classified, Inc.—676 N. St. Clair, Chicago, IL 60611

How to Predict (Quickly) Ad Response

It helps the mail dealer to be able to predict advertising results quickly. This allows time to resubmit ads to all media that are "working."

Following is a predicting method that, while not 100% accurate, serves as a good barometer:

DAILY NEWSPAPERS: ½ of total response will be reached within 3 days of receiving your first order or inquiry.

WEEKLY NEWSPAPERS OR MAGAZINES: ½ of total response will be reached within 6 days of receiving your first order or inquiry.

MONTHLIES: ½ of your total response will be reached within 14 days of receiving your first order or inquiry.

BI-MONTHLIES: ½ of your total response will be reached within 22 days of receiving your first order or inquiry.

I have found this rule applies to either display or classified advertising.

The bottom line is always your chief concern. Even when using the two-step inquiry approach, it is how many orders that are ultimately generated that makes or breaks your overall advertising approach.

All About Circulation

Your ad cost per 1,000 readers is an important consideration. Next to selecting the "right" publications for your ads, you want the most cost-effective advertising.

Example: If you're paying $1,500 for a full-page ad in a magazine that has a circulation of 100,000, you are paying $15 per 1,000 circulation.

If you pay $3000 to reach a 300,000 circulation, you are paying only $10 per 1,000 circulation. A substantial difference.

Always learn a publication's true circulation. Don't be misled by "readership" claims. Publishers tend to greatly inflate their possible "readership."

Moneysworth often makes claims of "five million readers," yet official circulation audit figures put *Moneysworth*'s actual circulation at about 800,000. Now *Moneysworth* has a proven record as an excellent place for many types (especially business opportunities) of mail advertising. It's just that they want you to believe five or six different people, on the average, read every issue that they print and mail. Methinks Publisher Ginzburg may be a bit optimistic!

Many publishers inflate their readership by three to six times actual circulation. It's a common practice, but one that, in my opinion, over-estimates their correct circulation and readership.

The type of circulation a publication has can also help you in making your advertising decisions.

72

The more copies a publication sends out by mail (subscriptions and samples), the more responsive it is likely to be for your mail order advertising. Newsstand buyers, as a whole, are not nearly as likely to be mail order buyers as folks who receive their publications by mail.

Reviewing a copy of Standard Rate and Data or Ayer Directory of Publications (both available at most libraries) will help you select suitable publications for your ad budget. This directory will also give you vital readership demographics, circulation figures and other hard facts (not inflated ad claims) that will help you in your advertising media selection process.

After everything is said and done, it is the bottom line (Did your ad pull enough response to earn a profit?) that will separate the "right and wrong" media for you. However, you should have your eyes wide open from the start. You can only benefit by getting a "feel" from looking through a sample copy of every publication you are considering as an advertising vehicle. You should also have updated and actual circulation figures to help you make an advertising decision.

First-time Ads Usually Pull Best

Since the same ad repeated in various publications generally will not pull as well as the first insertion, I strongly recommend you place your ads on a "one-time basis" in all untested media.

This is almost always true when placing large "direct order" space ads (many types of inquiry ads will produce steady results over many insertions and may be run for months, even years with little or no changes).

The fall-off for cash-up-front direct orders from the larger display ad is usually at least 10% and sometimes as high as 50% on every consecutive repeat.

The fall-off will always be higher from publications which have a majority of readers as subscribers than those which have a high sample copy (as is the case with newsstand publications) readership. Many of the sales/opportunity magazines constantly mail to new lists, thus the fall-off is substantially reduced.

Mail dealers advertising specialized courses, soliciting salesmen, etc., often run their ads for several months or years, issue-after-issue, in various media, while operators selling a specific book, gift item or other type consumer product seldom can make the proposition pay beyond two or three consecutive insertions, and the first insertion is almost always the best puller.

If your ad pulls well in an April issue and is marginally profitable in the May issue of a publication, it would probably be wise to drop out of that medium, at least until October or November, at which time you may wish to retest.

Joe Karbo found that even in the best media for his "Lazy Man's Way to Riches" ads, he had to stagger his advertising to keep profits up.

The only media he dared use more than three or four times in one year was a select group of daily newspapers. The Sunday *Los Angeles Times* pulled so well for his book offer that he ran large space ads one Sunday out of each month for long periods of time.

(your letterhead)

Advertising Director
ABC Magazine
New York, NY

Your publication is being considered as an
advertising medium for our new 300-page
manual, **Making Money for Yourself.**

Please forward your media package to include
an ABC statement of circulation, your readership
demographics, a recent sample copy and an
advertising rate card. Would you like us to send
you a review copy of this new soft-cover book?

Please place us on file to be notified of future
rate or policy changes. Thank you.

Sincerely,

(Your name)

Sample letter to receive sample copy and state of circulation, rates, etc., from any publication.

Remnant Space Advertising

Most magazines today are offset printed (from camera-ready copy) in press signatures of four or eight pages. If a magazine is working with a printer who uses, for example, eight-page signatures, he must conform by submitting 80 pages, 88 pages, etc. 81 to 87 pages won't work.

Although magazines are pasted-up well in advance of their "on sale date," a publisher who comes up with an "odd number of pages" needs filler quickly.

Using the above example, let's say Mr. Publisher finds himself with 84 ready-to-print pages. That's four too many or four too few for the combination of eight-page signatures his printer requires. (Of course, the amount could be 76, 92 or any amount that did not include even multiples of 8 pages.)

Since he is not about to cut back the number of pages by 4 (unless he had 4 pages of editorial fillers or public service notices he felt were expendable), he will go after 4 more pages—quickly. An extra article or many fillers and announcements could do the trick. However, they won't produce revenue.

A desire for more ad revenue to fill blank pages may lead our publisher to offer some ad space at substantial discounts.

Most of the "heavy hitters" in mail order advertising buy a large portion of their space ads at discounts far below the prices quoted on the publishers' various rate cards. They obtain discounts by contracting to buy a large amount of ad space months or even years in advance or by letting certain publishers know they have both camera-ready ads (usually full-page ads are required) and cash money on hand to cover a "fast insertion" in the publisher's magazine.

Remnant ad space is not seeking the rank beginner. However, once you begin to build a solid mail order operation and have enough cash on hand to handle, and suitable copy to quickly accept, cut-rate advertising offers (discounts run from 20% to 50%), you can begin to contact various publishers. Obviously, you should only contact media that is suited for the books you are selling.

I do not wish to lead you to think that all publishers make remnant deals. Some do and some don't! However, you'll be surprised how many do, under certain conditions, when they know you have ad copy and cash money and are ready to take quick action.

How to Establish
Your Own Advertising Agency

The next best thing to remnant space discount advertising is taking an agency discount of 15% to 17% off regular rates on all advertising you place.

How do you do it? Simple! Establish your own advertising agency!!

It really is quite simple to set up your own ad agency, and if you use a fair amount of space, savings will be considerable.

Here's the easy, step-by-step procedure:

1. Use a name different than your regular mail order company name. If you're simply using your own name to sell by mail, use some variation for your agency name. Example: John Miller Sales could start an agency as J.M. Advertising. If your company name is Mid-America Book Company, perhaps Mid-West Advertising could serve as your "agency name."

2. Register and license your ad agency name if your state requires this.

3. Have a local printer run off a couple hundred "Insertion Order" sheets (you may copy the form I have reprinted here. Type in your new agency name under "Agency").

4. Submit all of your future advertising to the media by using the "Insertion Order" form, deducting 15% from their rate cards. Most publishers also allow agencies an extra 1% or

2% for sending cash with order.

Discounts of 15% to 17% can amount to a tidy sum over a year of advertising. Money saved is money earned! Isn't it time you established your own advertising agency? Who knows, in addition to saving plenty of money on your own advertising, from time to time others may request that you place orders for them. It won't cost them a penny more, and you then could pocket up to 17% for just handling the transactions.

My own advertising agency was started just to save me money on my own space advertising, but over the years I have earned extra profits by placing ads for various copywriting clients. It is an added bonus to setting up your own ad agency to save money on your own ads.

INSERTION ORDER

AGENCY: TO:

PRODUCT: DATE:

ADVERTISER:

dates of insertion	number of times	caption to read	key or code	space ordered

COPY TO READ:

SPECIAL INSTRUCTIONS & REQUESTS:

RATE:

_____times at $_____   Less____% frequency discount $_____
= $_____   Less____% agency commission $_____
Check #_____   Less____% cash discount $_____
By:_____   Net amount of this order $_____

Newspaper Space Advertising

Newspaper space (display) advertising does not work for every type of mail order product or book ad, but when it does work, it can be s-u-p-e-r! Ads in most publications take weeks or months before they appear. With newspapers, your ad can be in print within a couple of days—*lightning-fast results!*

A major key to success with a newspaper space ad is position. The main reason folks don't respond to newspaper ads is: *they don't see them!* With major dailies averaging around 100 pages weekdays, and up to 300 or more pages in Sunday editions, friend, your ad can get lost in such overwhelming verbage.

Almost nobody (save some glutton for punishment) is going to read the entire paper. Few people read more than two or three sections. A man may want the front pages and sports section. A lady might zero in on the local news section and the food section. A kid may dig for the comics. Entrepreneurs and investors may seek the business section. Gossip mongers want the society pages, and Nancy Reagan hunts for the astrological charts (just kidding!).

While most folks don't read all the sections in a paper, much less the whole thing, almost everyone touches and glances at the front of the paper. Thus, the best place for your ad is the front of a section. The second best place is the back of a section. The third best place for your ad is in the section most likely to be read by the guy or gal who will want your book.

Example: Business or moneymaking book ads do best in either the financial section or in the sports pages. Reason: Although more and more women are getting involved in moneymaking ventures, over 80% of business/money book buyers are men. Most guys read the financial pages. Almost all men (92%) who read newspapers read the sports section.

Once you have good position, the next thing is to grab and hold reader attention. A good, solid headline and an ad that looks and reads like a news story will work best in a newspaper.

Make your ad read like an "article." Editorial material (or an ad dressed up like an editorial) will always get far more readership than does an ad that looks like an ad.

Newspapers are loaded with hundreds of ads that shout "I'm an ad!" But, do people obtain newspapers to read ads? Of course not. They want articles, stories, and editorials. Make your ad get read by making it look like the stuff they want to read. The more readers you hook, the more orders you'll land!

Direct mail lets
you target market.

DIRECT MAIL ADVERTISING

Direct mail is a multi-billion-dollar method of doing business that has experienced phenomenal growth in the United States during the past 20 years. A recent (Spring, 1988) severe rate increase in postal rates (particularly hard hit was the third class/bulk mail basic increase from 12.5¢ per piece, to 16.7¢ per piece) has slowed down—but by no means stopped—direct mail advertising. Many industry leaders are hoping that increased competition, through private mail delivery, will eventually provide relief from the United States Postal Service, which spends 80% to 85% of all revenues on a labor force—making its workers the highest paid semi-skilled employees in the world.

Go First Class

The most recent 1988 postal increases illustrate the U.S.P.S.' continuing "war on bulk mailers." Basic third class single piece bulk mail rate escalated from 12.5 cents to 16.7 cents. A staggering, *what are they doing to us* increase of *more than 30%!* While many officials with the Postal Service concede that bulk advertising mail helps keep the whole system afloat, they now increase the rates to a point that threatens the survival of many of their best customers—mail order companies, catalog houses, and mail order booksellers—both large and small.

The previous 1985 postal increases of all classifications of mail were mild compared to the 1988 bulk mail hike. In the past, large and small bulk mailers complained for a short spell, and then went about business as usual, dramatically increasing bulk mailings by over 15% during the past 2½ years. However, this recent increase is far more severe.

This time it will be different. The latest bulk rate mail increase is far too severe. *Carnage* is a better description.

Faster mail service and deliverability could soften the blow a little, but this seems unlikely. In recent months service seems to be slower, and deliverability appears to be declining. The trade publication *DM News* recently reported that the major mailers who closely monitor deliverability of their third class bulk offering have been complaining about non-deliverability in the 13% to 25% range. Imagine that! Up to 250 pieces out of every 1,000 mailed never reach their destination. *Scary stuff, eh?* What can a mail order company publisher, or merchandise or information seller, who wants to "survive and thrive," (and survival is the first cause of concern!) do? GO FIRST CLASS!!

The latest increase of a first class stamp from 22¢ to 25¢ was modest, compared to the irresponsible bulk rate increase. Also, the speed and deliverability of first class mailings is near-perfect, when compared to all other mail classifications. True, 25¢ per piece is still substantially more than 16.7¢ per piece, but when you consider all factors—speed of delivery, a very low non-deliverability factor, no charge for "nixies" (mail improperly addressed, or mail returned when folks have moved), plus the time and effort of sorting and bundling and maintaining lists in zip code order—I believe first class mail now makes sense. If you can keep weight from exceeding one ounce, go first class. Truly at the mercy of the U.S.P.S., it would be pretty hard to justify paying 45¢ per piece for each two-ounce piece of mail, as opposed to the 16.7¢ basic rate—even with all the problems associated with bulk mail.

Become weight conscious! I have been able to take several direct mail pieces that weighed a little more than one ounce and decrease them to a little less than one ounce by using lighter-weight paper stock. Talk it over with your printer.

Consider all your advertising options. If your tests indicate direct mail works best for you—as it does for several dealers—consider seriously my case for reducing weight, and going first class!

Mailing Lists

At the center of any direct mail effort is the mailing list you use. Powerful copywriting, expert printing, good graphics, etc., are very important, but mailing lists are the heart of any direct mail effort.

Mailing lists fall under three categories:

(1) In-house lists
(2) Mail response lists
(3) Compiled lists

A dealer's own in-house list is by far the firm's most precious commodity. These are the people who have ordered or inquired at least once. Within the in-house list, at the very core, are the company's "family jewels"—the multiple buyers—the best of all the house names.

The mail response lists are names who have responded to another company's offer. There are several thousands of such lists, in all fields and classifications, available on the mailing list rental market, including hundreds of different lists of mail order book buyers and opportunity seekers. Standard Rate & Data Services, Inc., 3004 Glenview Road, Willmette, IL 60091, publishes the "mailing list bibles" for both business lists and consumer lists in the "Direct Mail Lists, Rates and Data Directories." In thumbing through their huge directories, you will find many thousands of both response and compiled lists in almost any classification you could possibly think of, as well as many that probably never entered your mind.

Compiled lists are generally not as "responsive" as lists generated from actual orders and inquiries. I do not recommend the use of compiled lists for the purpose of selling books by mail. 99% of the time they won't work.

One big factor concerning all types of mailing lists (yours, theirs or compiled) is recency. After you build your own list, mail to it at least three times or more per year. When possible, mail to rented response lists that are new on the list market or which have recently been cleaned. Clean names (with most undeliverables—called "nixies"—removed) are also vitally important. Of course, any response list that has worked well for books similar to the ones you sell will probably work for you too.

Your own mailing list can also be a chief source of additional revenue. The main purpose of your in-house list—customers or inquiries—is to generate follow-up business. A profitable secondary use of these lists is income obtained from renting your names to other mail order dealers. Profits from renting your names to other companies can be very substantial. A list renting for $60 per thousand will yield $48 to you, after paying the normal 20% brokerage fee. With some mail order operations, capital received from renting their own customer lists represents a major part of overall profits.

Trading your customer list with another mail order book company can also be an excellent way to achieve more direct mail business. In trading with a competitor, be certain you are trading like-for-like. If you are furnishing 5,000 recent buyers, you want 5,000 of their recent buyers in exchange, not a list of two-year-old buyers or a list of inquiries only.

Since there is a degree of "flim-flam" in the mailing list business, it is often wise to do all of your buy, sell and trade list business through a reputable broker.

(A list of brokers I believe to be—but cannot guarantee—reputable is found in the *Source Directory*, in the back section of this book.)

Predicting Direct Mail Results

In looking over many first class and fourth class bulk mail records, I have come up with my prediction timetable:

First Class Mail: ½ of all orders that you will receive will be reached within 6 days of the first day you receive orders.

Fourth Class Bulk: ½ of all orders that you will receive will be reached within 18 days of the first day you receive orders.

Although orders from first class mail will trickle in over many months and fourth class mail results can drag on for a year or more, I have found the above timetable to be 98% accurate. Don't confuse the first day you receive orders with the day you mail. For example, you may receive your first orders on a first class direct mailing six days after the day you mail. This would mean 12 days total would pass before you reached ½ of your total response of this mailing.

These results are based on a nationwide mailing. Results will come much faster if your mailing is local or regional only.

The Standard Direct Mail Format

Letters

1. First in importance in the direct format is the letter (remember: direct mail is supposed to be one-to-one, personal advertising). The letter can be one page or many pages. The key is to use as many words as needed to sell your offer, but no more than necessary. Keep it friendly, personal, enthusiastic, with no hard sell, but do ask for that book order.

2. One of the most popular and proven mailing pieces consists of an outside envelope, letter, circular, order card and reply envelope.

3. All important sentences should be highlighted by bold type, caps, italics or underlining.

4. A two, three, or four-page letter usually has more pulling power than a one-page letter.

5. A neatly typed "personal style" letter usually is more effective than a professional-looking typeset letter.

Circulars

1. A professional-looking circular (typeset with photos and/or art work) is usually the best way to support a personalized letter that contains no photos or art work.

2. The more expensive your offer is, the more professional-looking your circular (but not your letter) should be.

Outside envelopes

1. While a combination of larger or smaller sizes of

envelopes have proven to be effective for various offers, the standard size No. 10 works best for most.

2. Teaser copy that relates to the copy inside usually increases response.

Reply Envelopes

1. Any reply envelope generally increases results.

2. Postage-free reply envelopes will often outpull those that require your customer to affix a stamp.

Order Card or Form

1. A separate order form will usually outpull one that is printed on your circular that needs to be cut out.

2. An order form with an "official" looking guarantee will usually outpull one that simply states a guarantee.

Postage

1. Postage-metered or stamped envelopes often will outpull a pre-printed permit.

2. First class mail commands more attention than any other classification, and its deliverability rate is also the best. If your mailing piece is less than one ounce, consider going first class. If your mailing piece is over one ounce, a bulk-rate mailing, even with all its problems—slow deliverability and some no-deliverability—is probably more cost effective.

Incoming Mail

With either space, classified or direct mail advertising, the morning mail should be picked up early if you receive it from a rented post office box. If you have it delivered to your home or office address, you are at the mercy of your mail carrier. In either case, here is a method that you, your spouse or someone who works for you can use to handle the day's mail.

1. Open all mail.

2. Sort mail into piles of (a) orders, (b) inquiries, (c) bills, (d) advertising and (e) "white mail."

Let me digress to make sure you understand the five categories. Orders and/or standard inquiries would be response from direct mailings or space ads. Bills would be invoices to you from suppliers, equipment rental firms, utility companies, etc. Advertising is offers sent you from other mail order dealers. "White mail" is letters from buyers or inquiries that require personal attention and a specific answer not found in your regular sales literature.

3. Type labels from orders and/or inquiries. Use multiple carbon sheets and "key" each label so that you know exactly what was ordered and the date.

Example:

> 070288-TS
> Carol Thompson
> 120 N. Magnolia Ave.
> El Cajon, CA 92020

This would tell us that on July 2, 1988 (070288), Carol Thompson ordered my book—*How to Achieve Total Success* (TS). There are simpler and more complex ways to code, but this example should give you the general idea.

4. To "stay ahead" of your incoming mail, it is wise to pre-package orders and inquiry mail. In this way it is ready for postage and labeling and fast turnaround.

5. Place the extra carbon copies of the labels, or make photo copies, on index cards and file (in the case of a two-step inquiry ad program, you may wish to set up a follow-up

system). Let's say your program required three follow-ups after the original mailing, spaced 14 days apart. Using two file folders to cover a two month span can accomplish this. If an inquiry is received, let's say, October 14, then we would include an October 28 label in our October folder and two labels (11/11 and 11/25) in the November folder.

6. Take care of your "white mail" by answering questions, settling complaints, etc.

7. Go through the advertising you received. Handle and release everything in one of three ways: (a) place an order for something you want or need that will help your business, (b) file for future reference—supply catalogs, etc.—or (c) throw it away.

Anyone in mail order selling for any length of time knows it is all too easy to get bogged down with stacks of mail. This can create a real problem. To avoid getting behind on your business mail, take care of your mail handling responsibilities daily.

You can lose valuable repeat business by taking too long to fill orders or inquiries (a 48-hour or less turnaround is good business practice), and you can even get yourself into hot water with the post office and other consumer agencies if you're extremely tardy filling orders. The law now requires that all orders be filled within 30 days or the customer be sent an explanation as to when it will be filled, along with the option for the customer to get a full refund if he or she does not want to wait any longer.

My policy has always been to ship all orders received from customers or dropship orders from our dealers within 24 hours. Fast service greatly increases repeat business, and repeat sales are vital to mail order success.

Stay Friendly With Your
Local Post Office

It will pay you real dividends to have an amicable relationship with everyone who works at your local post office.

Although postal workers are supposed to treat everyone impartially, I have seen "preferred service" given to customers well-liked by postal employees. And on an occasion or two, yours truly has received some extra-special care.

Post Office Box or Street Address?

"Nobody can live in a little post office box and customers know this. They prefer dealing with folks who use a regular street address."

The above gospel has been preached by many mail order pros for a long, long time. While I won't call it totally bad advice, I do believe the times and attitudes have changed a lot in recent years. A postal box gives you the best service. Mail will usually reach a P.O. box one day sooner than a residence or office. Also, inside a post office you can handle all your mailing and postage needs.

If you do use a P.O. box exclusively, it may be a good idea to list your phone number in your ads, and your phone number should always be used on your sales letters. This tells customers you are very reachable. Mail order customers like to believe they are dealing with "real live people" who will be responsive to their orders or requests for more information, etc. The "closer" they feel to you, the more apt they are to favor you with their business.

Always Offer a Money-Back Guarantee

Mail order customers expect you to offer a guarantee. For most dealers, overall returned merchandise is quite low. Nevertheless, a Money Back Guarantee is of real importance. It instills confidence in the potential buyer. It tells him or her that you aim to please and that you won't take the money and run. A 30-day return guarantee is most often used by mail order dealers, but even a short 10-day guarantee is far better than no guarantee.

In recent years, several large mail dealers have begun to employ a very special guarantee whereby the customer's check or money order is held uncashed for 30 days. Joe Karbo, a very innovative mail order book peddler, originated this unique guarantee enroute to earning millions on a very popular book titled "The Lazy Man's Way to Riches." In recent years dozens of others have copied this approach. Joe was a real pro and a true genius in selling books by mail. Still, I do not recommend this approach for the "just getting started in mail order book selling" entrepreneur. In the early stages of mail selling, your cash flow is going to be vital and you'll probably need to bank every dollar the same day it arrives at your home, office or post office box.

Remember, any kind of guarantee is better than no guarantee. Treat your customers well and they will help you build and expand your mail order book business.

Repeat orders from satisfied buyers is a major success factor, and only happy customers will favor you with repeat business.

Direct Mail Success Guidelines

Over twenty years in this crazy, wonderful, often misunderstood business has taught me a lot about what works and what does not. Since I practice what I preach on a daily basis (never trust marketing advice from anyone who is not a front-line, battle-scarred veteran), I teach from experience, and not a textbook of theory.

Presented here, in random order, are some truths and

guidelines that can deliver direct mail success.

- Your mailing piece should be primarily aimed at your prospect's emotions. Intellectual considerations come second.

- Your sales letter is the most important component in your direct mail package.

- Long sales letters (well written and benefit-laden) usually outpull short letters. Four pages will almost always beat two, and six or eight pages may work even better.

- Sales letters should be black ink on white paper.

- Copy must be filled with benefits, and also be believable. Good salesmanship in print. Written on a one-to-one basis.

- Wide margins increase readership.

- Typewritten copy for your sales letter usually works best. However, a large, typeset headline, followed by typewritten copy works well for many offers.

- Your best copy should come early in the letter, and the offer should be mentioned early on.

- Short words, sentences, and paragraphs work best. Underlining, used moderately, can enhance results. Above all else, copy must be interesting.

- There is NO stronger word in copy than *FREE.*

- Premiums (free bonuses) almost always increase response. Premiums usually work better than price discounts.

- "Buck slips" that explain discounts or premiums are very helpful. A strong P.S. is a must. It always gets attention.

- Endorsements are effective. Full names are much more effective than the use of just initials.

94

- Self-mailers seldom work as well as using envelopes.

- Number 10 business envelopes usually work better than larger (or smaller) sizes.

- Window envelopes often will outpull a regular envelope.

- A return envelope is essential. A prepaid B.R.E. often will outpull a regular B.R.E., but the added cost often does not warrant its use.

- A separate order card will most likely outpull an order coupon that is printed on a letter or circular.

- First class mail sometimes is so responsive as to warrant its use, but only for pieces that weigh under one ounce.

- Teaser copy on envelopes works for some offers, but no teaser copy also works well for other promotions.

- A strong, money-back guarantee always encourages more orders.

- A strong brochure or circular will usually increase response. Your important benefits should appear in both your brochure and your sales letter.

- Graphics, art work, and typesetting is recommended for brochures or circulars, but not letters.

- Sweepstake offers will usually increase response 40% to 100%.

- Granting credit (we'll bill you later!) will usually increase response by 60-120%.

- Sweepstakes and credit increases response dramatically, but the cost of prizes and the cost and headaches of trying to collect from credit buyers often negates their effectiveness.

- Lift letters can lift response by 10%, making them very cost-effective.

- Retail store prices ($39.95 instead of $40.00) almost always works best.

- Use the very best copywriters available.

- Shop for *price, quality and service* from suppliers. All three are vital to your success.

- Be a real professional. Sell only items you would appreciate owning at prices you would be willing to pay. Ship promptly. Use every legal ploy to get the business, and then offer the great service, information, and fairness that will make them want to continue doing business with you.

- Fulfillment is both a responsibility and a customer-building department. In most cases, orders should be processed and shipped within 48 hours of receipt. Fast, efficient fulfillment builds customer confidence, respect and satisfaction—key ingredients for your continued success in mail marketing.

- Set up and maintain a strong record-keeping apparatus. Know at a glance in which direction your business is heading.

- Discover the "dollar value" of every customer you obtain. This information is available by analyzing the "average" ordering characteristic of your present customer base.

- The mailing list you use is the single most important factor of any direct mail campaign.

- Response (proven mail order buyers) lists almost always out-pull compiled lists.

- Your own customers represent the most responsive list you can use.

- Stay in touch with your customers—no less than four mailings per year, all offering related items.

- Your customers are very special. Treat them like you

would like to be treated, only better! Excel in fair dealing and friendly, fast service. Do this and you will be greatly rewarded with increased business.

"Hot Line" Mailing Lists Will Work Best

The "hot line" list is a company's most recent buyer's name. In most cases that means buyers within the most recent 90-day period. Obviously, these names will be the most responsive.

If a company has a recent 10,000 "hot line" and a "main list" of 100,000, we should test the hot line first. If it doesn't work for us, the bigger main list most certainly won't either.

On the other hand, if the hot line pulls well for us, we must consider that there will be a drop-off in response once we begin using names from the master file.

Example: let's say we mail to the 10,000 hot line and obtain a 2% response (2 orders for every 100 direct mail pieces we mail). Rather than a gung-ho mailing to the entire big mail list of 100,000 older names (all of which will be many months to many years old, although hopefully recently cleaned and updated), we would do well to test only 5,000 or 10,000 names from that company's main mailing list, realizing that response probably won't be as favorable as from its recent hot line names.

Over the years I have noted the drop off in response percentage between hot line and older names averages between 20% and 30%. Thus a 2% return from hot line names will probably fall to around 1.5% once we begin using the company's larger, and older, mail list. That's a big difference! A 25% drop in response percentage could turn a profitable direct mail campaign into a losing one. Only through tests will we know.

Cheap Lists—Big Money Wasted!

The going rate for mailing lists most likely to be rented by information sellers (opportunity seekers, book buyers, etc.) is currently $50-$75 per 1,000 names. Beware of lists costing less! Everyone likes a bargain, but I could fill many pages in this book with horror stories of mail dealers who have used "cheap lists." Beware of those little ads in magazines (or larger ads) that offer names at bargain basement prices.

Not all cheap lists are worthless, but the vast majority of them are. A company or mailing list broker who is peddling names at a big discount is often offering old response names, questionably compiled names, and/or over-used names. 99 times out of 100 that spells disaster!

The names you use will always be just a small part of the total cost of your mailing. Postage and printed matter costs will always take the biggest bite out of any direct mail budget. Don't be penny wise and dollar foolish is the cliche that applies here.

You don't save money by using a cheap mailing list, you *lose* money!

Since there are many highly suspect mailing lists out there, plus more than a little "flim-flam" in the list business, it is generally a good idea to do all your mailing list business through reputable brokers, and not with someone who runs a little ad in a magazine, offering great prices on mailing lists.

Direct mail is a one-to-one medium that lets you reach a select target market. To be successful, you must use a good list.

PROFITABLE MARKETING

All successful mail order information sellers have one thing in common: they have learned how to market what they sell or have hired a skillful direct response professional (copywriter/consultant) to help them *shake the money tree*. Here, in random order, is a series of my articles on marketing (advertising, copy, promotions, etc.) that may be of help to you. Some of the following writings first appeared in my newsletter, *Information Marketing Success.* *

Information Marketing Success is written and edited by Russ von Hoelscher, and published by Publishers Media. A sample copy is available for $2 from: Publishers Media, Dept. M, PO Box 546, El Cajon, CA 92022.

There's a fine line between success and failure (and lots of money is only one measure of success). A positive self-image, plus positive action is vital to achieve. Believe! Act!! Achieve!!!

Benefit Copy: *Pushing Their Buttons—Not Yours!*

"How do you like my new brochure, Russ?" he asked, and before I could answer, the noted public speaker beamed and added, "it's a real beauty!" Indeed it was. Very colorful. A four-color, well-printed, 2-sided, 11x17 that folded down to four 8½x11 pages. On page one, the subject was standing in a woodsy, outdoor setting with his eyes gazing toward the heavens. Bold copy stated: *A MAN FOR ALL SEASONS.* Opening the brochure to page 2, here was a full page blowup of our subject again, this time holding a mike in his hand. Sadly, the copy here was all too predictable: *A SPEAKER FOR ALL OCCASIONS.*

Pages 3 and 4 of his expensive brochure expounded on his past achievements, his educational background, and his views on how to create a healthier, sane, happier world. Almost as an afterthought, on the bottom portion of page 4, he mentioned that his speaking topics included health, exercise and nutrition, and that he had also authored a book on these subjects.

"How do you like this brochure," he repeated.

"Your fan club will love it," I answered. Sometimes I am more candid than I am discreet. While the above may appear to be an extreme case of far too much self and far too few reader benefits in advertising and sales literature, unfortunately that is not the case. At least 90% of all ads, brochures, and sales letters that I review are very heavy on self-glorification (the person, the book, the seminar, the service or the product) and very light on benefits to the potential reader, attendee or user. That's dumb. It's also ineffective. While some mention of yourself, your company, and how great your product is may be appropriate (especially if it is done in the right way—to instill trust and confidence), the vast majority of all copy should be benefit copy. Who cares how famous, important, rich or smart you are? What potential responders really care about is how happy, popular, important, wealthy, healthy, better-looking or brilliant they can become by using what you have to offer. They want and crave benefits. Forget you—the important question is: what's in it for me?

People aren't anxious to buy anything.
However, they will gladly spend money
to obtain real or imagined benefits.

Here are ten great ways to make your ads and mailings more responsive:

1. *State a primary benefit in your headline* (ads, brochures) or your opening paragraph in letters. Capture your reader's attention quickly by telling him or her something very good he/she can easily obtain from you.

2. *Make it believable.* This is the age of great skepticism. Trust is not readily available, and to overcome this fact, you must explain why so much good is possible to those who respond. How do you do this? Stress benefits! Big benefits first, but then lots of little benefits. Always remember, a small benefit (to you) could be a big benefit to your reader.

3. *Be specific.* Spell out exactly what benefits are being offered. It's always more productive to state "You can make $50,000 a year with this home-based business," than to merely say, "You can make big money at home with this business opportunity." "Look and feel ten years younger in ninety days," is much stronger than saying, "You'll look and feel younger in a short period of time." Be exact. Use time, dates, amounts, etc.

4. *You must understand what people really want.* Example: You are offering a short course on learning to play the guitar. Your target market is young males who like music. Learning to play the guitar for self-gratification is just one, very obvious benefit your potential customer wants. Other benefits most likely include: Popularity (his friends will appreciate him more), Sex Appeal (young ladies often get turned on by music and to those who can play it), and Self-Esteem (expertly playing a musical instrument probably will make him have a much higher image of himself). As you can see, it's very likely that much more than mastering a musical skill is involved in deciding if he should send for this course. By considering all potential buyer motivations, you can push the right buttons, regardless of what you are offering.

5. *Include testimonials.* Your claims are just that—they're your claims. Testimonials add substance. What others say about your book, product or service is often more convincing than what you say. Use as many testimonials as you can obtain, and when authorized to do so, use complete names. Full names instill more buyer confidence than the use of only initials.

6. *Use only artwork and photos that show benefits.* Graphic art and/or photographs can be a big plus in your sales literature, but only if they complement your copy. Use them to demonstrate benefits. Obviously, if you're a public speaker, a professional photo of yourself is important. But even then, don't load up your brochure with self-photos at the expense of benefit copy. Anyone who fills up space with several photos of himself has both an ego problem and printed salesmanship that has been weakened.

7. *Think and write you, not I.* Good copy is always "you" copy. And copy that does not contain at least twice as many you's as I's is not stressing enough benefits.

8. ***Always include a personalized letter.*** Your beautiful brochure may turn you on, and you may consider it the highlight of your mailing package. Nevertheless, for best results always include a "personalized" (even if mass-produced) letter with each package you mail. A letter almost always increases your response. It allows you to talk benefits, one on one.

9. ***Summarize your offer and its benefits.*** The last paragraph of your ads or letters should briefly and concisely summarize your offer and its strongest points.

10. ***Add a "Bonus Benefit" for a prompt response.*** People love to get a little extra for their money. If at all possible, offer a free bonus. This almost always increases results. Your freebie need not be an expensive item, but it should be something likely to appeal to the tastes or lifestyle of your readers.

How to Write a Successful Direct Mail Sales Letter

Through careful mailing selection, direct mail can give you specific selectivity unmatched in any other advertising medium. In any direct marketing format that you decide to use, your sales letter is of primary importance. Presented here are tips that should help you write an attention-grabbing sales letter.

FIRST THINGS FIRST

Before you begin writing your direct mail letter, you must know:

1. Your target market—who you want to reach

2. What appeal is most likely to motivate these people

3. The most important benefits of your product or service

4. Exactly what action you want your reader to take (write for more information, call, send in the order, etc.)

5. Your budget

6. Your competition and what they are promoting

7. What mailing list to use. The list you use is very important. Your good sales letter must go to a responsive audience.

18 SURE STEPS TO WRITING A GOOD SALES LETTER

(1) Use a Strong Lead Statement: This is extremely important. We want to quickly capture our reader's attention. If we don't succeed in doing this, he may toss our letter aside after a brief glance. The best leads are (not necessarily in this order): (A) News. If your product or service is really news, this is a great lead. (B) How/what/why; the classic newspaper approach. (C) The numbered ways, such as ten ways this service will improve your life. (D) Narrative. This approach is difficult for many to write, but a good story can capture the reader's attention. (E) A provocative question will also usually arouse curiosity and interest. (F) A bold statement. A bold, unusual or even shocking statement (make certain it's true!) will almost always get the reader involved.

(2) Stress Benefits: Don't waste much time or words on telling your reader how great you are (although a few favorable lines about yourself/your company may be in order); instead promise many, many benefits—the more benefits the better. List the major benefits first, but follow up with minor benefits. A minor benefit to you may be a major one to your reader.

(3) Keep the Copy Tight: If you wish to present only a one-page letter, write at least two pages and then delete needless words. There is strong evidence that a two-, three- or four-page sales letter will out-perform a one-pager, however, the copy must be tight. Nobody wants a full history of your company or product/service. Good advice is to write twice as much copy as you will ultimately use and then edit it down to a flowing, strong presentation.

(4) Humor Doesn't Usually Work: There rarely is anything funny or beneficial about injecting humor into a sales letter. If you are called on to deliver a speech or oral sales presentation, a little humor can often work well. No so, in most cases, with a sales letter.

(5) Reinforce Your Letter with a Flyer or Brochure: An effective, attractive flyer or brochure allows you to present the benefits of your offer in another way.

(6) Make Your Letter "Personalized." Direct mail is the personal medium and your sales letter should make this true. A typed, "personal style" letter almost always is more effective than a slick, professional-looking, typeset letter. Your brochure or sales flyer probably should be typeset with the use of any appealing graphics. Just keep the letter itself personal.

(7) Don't Split Your Message: While some tell half the story in the letter and the other half in the brochure, you'll do much better by telling your whole story, with all the benefits, in both elements. Keep in mind, some readers will choose to read only one.

(8) Keep Sentences and Paragraphs Short: For maximum readability, keep most sentences to 12 words or less and paragraphs to no more than five or six lines. Whether it will

actually take just a couple of minutes or over ten minutes to read your message, many will not get involved unless your copy looks like "a fast, easy read."

(9) Offer a Freebie: People love to get a little extra for their money. If at all possible offer a free bonus. This almost always increases results. Your freebie need not be an expensive item, but it should be something likely to appeal to the tastes or lifestyle of your readers.

(10) Ask for Action from the Start: Don't be coy about it, let your reader know what you want him to do right from the beginning. Rephrase it from time to time. Point the reader in the direction of when you will ask him to order now.

(11) Use Testimonials: Whenever possible, include a few favorable testimonials. Be certain to use the other person's full name and affiliation. Using only initials will water down this powerful sales tool.

(12) Summarize your Offer: The last paragraph of your letter should briefly and concisely summarize your offer and its strongest points.

(13) A P.S. is a Must! With the possible exception of your salutation and opening paragraph, a P.S. will attract the strongest attention. Make it a solid and intriguing sales pitch.

(14) Ask for the Order: Don't beat around the bush. Both your closing paragraph and your P.S will attract the strongest attention. Make it a solid and intriguing sales pitch.

(15) Eliminate the Risk: Whenever possible, offer a strong guarantee, a free trial period, etc. A good place to inject a strong guarantee is early in your letter, and then reinforce it near the end of your letter.

(16) Include the Price: If you fear including the price it can only be because either your benefit package or guarantee may not be up to par. If your price is low, tell the reader so. If your price is high, make sure you have beefed up your benefit package.

(17) Ask for Immediate Action: When possible give a reason for quick response. Order within the next 30 days and receive a free gift; order before this date and receive a nice discount, etc.

(18) Make Sure Everything Flows and Reads Easily: Before you give your letter the final O.K., read it over several times, ask others to read it, and make certain it flows well and is both interesting and informative to read. Above all else, it must motivate positive action.

The No. 1 Factor for Achieving Mail Marketing Success

Above all else, do this. Treat your customers just like you would like to be treated, or even better! Satisfied customers will favor you more and repeat business is the major factor in achieving mail order success.

How to Prepare a Powerful Direct Mail Brochure
15 Dynamite Tips

(1) **Professionally typeset your brochure:** While it is often acceptable (even advisable) to type a letter, your brochure should be attractively typeset.

(2) **Use Appropriate Artwork or Photos:** Well presented artwork and/or photographs will usually enhance the appearance of your brochure.

(3) **Offer a Free Gift:** People love to receive a "free gift," and a free bonus will almost always increase the pulling power of your message.

(4) **Emphasize your Free Gift:** In both copy and illustration, play up the value of your valuable free gift.

(5) **Make it Colorful:** Full color usually increases response; however, even a two-color process brochure is more desirable than a one-color printing.

(6) **Make a Strong Claim, and Back it Up:** Direct mail buyers want benefits. Make a strong statement concerning benefits and back it up with support material.

(7) **Plain English, Please!** Don't let your copywriter try to impress the reader with his written verbiage. Keep it simple and easy to understand.

(8) **Use Copy and Design Professionals:** Use the very best copywriter and graphic artist available that you can afford. There is no substitute for good, creative talent.

(9) **A Risk-Free Offer Pulls Best:** Use a solid money-back

guarantee. Make sure the customer realizes he/she can order with confidence and that they will be satisfied.

(10) Consult Your Printer Early: Seek creative input from your printer during the planning stages. A good printer can help you design an attractive brochure and also make suggestions on ink and paper that could save you money.

(11) Content First, then Design: Before you determine how many pages your brochure should be (standard size is 11x17, folded to four 8½x11 pages), first decide how much information it will contain.

(12) What's the Competition Offering? Get every promotional package that your main competitors send out. In setting up a "swipe file" you'll have valuable information on what others in your field are doing. While you should not methodically copy their words or illustrations, they may give you a bright idea or two concerning how best to make your presentation.

(13) Talk to your Mailing List Broker Early: Since the mailing list you use in any direct mail promotion is the single most important factor, take care to select the best potential buyers list.

(14) Does your Brochure Flow and is it Easy to Read? Before setting type and pasting up the brochure, make any final copy or illustration changes deemed necessary. It must "flow" from point to point and be a "quick, enjoyable read" regardless of length.

(15) Use a Good Proofreader: Regardless of how good you are at proofreading, a sharp outside proofreader should be called in for the final reading.

SUPPLY SOURCES

Although we list here sources who we believe to be reliable and low-priced, Russ von Hoelscher and Profit Ideas cannot guarantee your satisfaction in dealing with individuals and companies. Comparison shopping is always recommended.

OFFSET PRINTERS

To print flyers, brochures, circulars, letterheads, etc. They can also print booklets, reports, and directories.

Henry Birtle Co.
1143 E. Colorado St.
Glendale, CA 91205

CNN Printing
PO Box 1751
Garden Grove, CA 92642

Creative Printing
309 S. Third St.
Ironton, OH 45638

MC Publishing & Printing
2002 London Rd., Rm. 101
Duluth, MN 55812

Nite & Day Printing
PO Box 700
Baldwin Park, CA 91706

Speedy Printers
23800 Aurora Rd.
Bedford Hts., OH 44146

Equitable Web Offset
24 New Bridge Rd.
Bergen Field, NJ 07621

Fitch Graphics
P.O. Box 768500
Atlanta, GA 30328

BOOK PRINTERS
Paperback or Hardback

Kingsport Press, Inc.
P.O. Box 711
Kingsport, TN 37662

McNaughton & Gunn, Inc.
P.O. Box M-2060
Ann Arbor, MI 48106

R.R. Donnelly & Sons
2223 Martin Luther King Dr.
Chicago, IL 60616

Book-Mart Press, Inc.
2001 Forty-Second St.
North Bergen, NJ 07047

Interstate Book Mfg.
2115 E. Kansas City Rd.
Olathe, KS 66061

Delta Lithograph Co.
14731 Califa St.
Van Nuys, CA 91411

Appollo Books Inc.
107 La Fayette St.
Winona, MN 55987

Thompson-Shore Inc.
7300 West Joy St.
Dexter, MI 48130

SELECT MAIL ORDER & BOOK TRADE PUBLICATIONS

Independent Publishers
  Marketing Report
P.O. Box 546
El Cajon, CA 92022
Sample copy, $2.00

Successful Opportunities
  National Publications
4580-B Alvarado Canyon Rd.
San Diego, CA 92120
Sample copy, FREE

Book Dealers World
P.O. Box 2525
La Mesa, CA 92041
Sample copy, $2.00

Towers Club Newsletter
P.O. Box 2038
Vancouver, WA 98668
Sample copy, $2.00

Making Profits Magazine
6255 Barfield Rd.
Atlanta, GA 30328
Sample copy, FREE

DM News
19 W. 21st St.
New York, NY 10010
Sample copy, FREE

Small Press Magazine
11 Ferry Lane, West
Westport, CT 06880
Sample copy, $3.50

Cosmep Newsletter
P.O. Box 703
San Francisco, CA 94101
Free sample newsletter on publishing/marketing books

HELP FROM A REAL-LIFE GHOST!

Thinking about doing a book, manual, newsletter, etc., but need help? Steve Lockman is a talented writer and ghostwriter. Quality work at a reasonable price. Write or call: Steve Lockman, PO Box 137, Lancaster, MN 56735, (218) 762-1341.

MAILING LIST BROKERS

Mega Media Assoc.
PO Box 4255
Balboa, CA 92661

Ed Burnett
99 W. Sheffield Ave.
Englewood, NJ 07631

List World
555 Sparkman Dr., –208, Rm 17
Huntsville, AL 35816

Trade Winds Co.
31 Tracy Rd.
New Paltz, NY 12561

Action Markets
1710 Highway 35
Ocean, NH 07712

Hank Marshall
P.O. Box 2729
Laguna Hills, CA 92653

Enterprise Lists
725 Market St.
Wilmington, DE 19801

Innovative Computer Technology
1245 Logan Ave.
Costa Mesa, CA 92626

SEMINARS & WORKSHOPS

Russ von Hoelscher offers all-day seminars several times each year on the topics of "Mail Order Success" and "Self-Publishing Success." Write for more information to: Russ von Hoelscher Seminars, Dept. S, PO Box 546, El Cajon, CA 92022.

SPECIAL NEWSLETTER OFFER

Publishers Media (PO Box 546, El Cajon, CA 92022) has many back issues of Russ von Hoelscher's *Freelance, IPN,* and *Words for Wealth* newsletters available. Good information for mail order booksellers and/or anyone thinking about self-publishing a book or manual. Special! 5 back issues (a reg. $15.00 value) for only $5.00 postpaid.

HOW-TO BOOKS FOR PUBLISHERS AND MAIL ORDER BOOK SELLERS

HOW YOU CAN MAKE A FORTUNE SELLING INFORMATION BY MAIL, by Russ von Hoelscher. Just recently published and already acclaimed *the definitive guide* on selling books and other "paper and ink" products (reports, manuals, directories, newsletters, etc.) through advanced mail order promotion methods. The small book you are now reading gives you important insights into making big money selling books by mail. This big new book tells you exactly how to do it, step by step. Now you will learn the *master strategies* and *professional techniques* that maximize mail order bookselling profits. Don't even consider self-publishing and/or mail order bookselling until you own and have read this revealing book, cover to cover. *How You Can Make a Fortune Selling Books by Mail* is available for only $12.95 plus $1.00 postage and handling, from: PROFIT IDEAS, 254 E. Grand Avenue, Escondido, CA 92025. (NOTE: This book plus five other great books, and all other dealership materials, will come to you if you send for the *Profit Ideas "FAST START" Dealers Kit*, the program that Russ von Hoelscher offers with his personal phone consultation and guidance.

HOW TO GET RICH IN MAIL ORDER, by my friend Melvin Powers, is loaded with dollar-doubling information and first-class strategies on how to make a fortune selling books and other forms of information by mail. Having sold nearly two hundred million books, most of them by mail, Melvin Powers has probably sold more books by mail order over the past forty years than any other source, except the Book of the Month Club. If you already have this great book, read it one more time for your sake. If you don't own a copy, get one at once. We'll rush you *How to Get Rich in Mail Order*, postpaid, by first class mail, for only $20. Order from: Publishers Media, Dept. MP, P.O. Box 546, El Cajon, CA 92022.

DIRECTORY OF LEADING MAGAZINES AND NEWSPAPERS. A valuable source manual of over 300 top-circulation American newspapers (plus some popular Canadian papers) and 700 leading consumer and trade magazines. The magazines listed cover all topics, with special emphasis given to business, sales and

114

financial publications. 1,000 great sources for mail order ads and free publicity, names and addresses, plus circulation data. This is a vital directory for mail order book dealers. Only $12 postpaid from Publishers Media, Dept. MN, P.O. Box 546, El Cajon, CA 92022.

BOOK DEALERS DROPSHIP DIRECTORY, by Al Galasso. Dropshipping enables you to sell books, collect payment in advance, then have the books shipped direct to your customers from the prime source. You carry no inventory. This directory lists hundreds of reliable dropship publishers. A great source guide! Order now for only $7.00 postpaid from: American Bookdealers Exchange, P.O. Box 2525-MM, La Mesa, CA 92041.

INTERNATIONAL WEALTH SUCCESS is a unique mail order monthly business opportunities newsletter covering capital sources, finder's fees, real estate, getting started in mail order, import-export, quick methods for raising money, venture capital, etc. Subscribers are entitled to run 12 free ads per year in the newsletter. Every issue is at least 16 pages and includes real-life experiences from Beginning Wealth Builders who are making their fortune today. Sample copy only $2.00 from: I.W.S., Inc., 24 Canterbury Rd., Rockville Centre, NY 11570.

MAKING $500,000 A YEAR IN MAIL ORDER, by David Bendah. This remarkable new mail order success book is unconditionally recommended by yours truly. Unlike many mail order trade books that cover the wide scope of mail selling, this big, new hardcover zeroes in on exactly how to make big money selling books by mail. Dave is a bright young man (he both publishes his own books and sells the Profit Ideas titles), and one of the fastest rising stars in the direct-marketing book business. More importantly to you, he is able to teach you his step-by-step success blueprint in this valuable new book. Available now for only $14.95 plus $1.00 postage/handling from: Lion Publishing Co., 6150 Mission Gorge Rd., Suite 222, San Diego, CA 92120.

THE HEALTH & WEALTH BUILDER is a 30-minute cassette tape that explains a unique network marketing opportunity with huge profit potential. This tape is **FREE** from: Direct Financial Service, 6925 5th Ave., E-184, Scottsdale, AZ 85251.

SMALL-TIME OPERATOR, by Bernard Kamoroff, C.P.A. This is one of the finest books ever written and published on the "Mechanics" of running a successful, small business. Subjects include: how to get started right and stay on target; how to set up your books and record-keeping system; how to deal effectively with employees; handle your tax responsibilities, and a whole lot more. The subject matter may appear dull, albeit necessary, but Mr. Kamoroff has accomplished the ultimate for a book of this nature. His information is crucial, and his writing style makes it come to life and capture our interest. Only $9.95 plus $1.00 postage from: Bell Springs Publishing, P.O. Box 640, Laytonville, CA 95454.

NATIONAL 75¢
ENQUIRER

30586-2   LARGEST CIRCULATION OF ANY PAPER IN AMERICA

Five Secrets That Could Make You a Millionaire

"You can become a millionaire if you know the right secrets," promises George Sterne, coauthor of *Secrets of the Millionaires: How Ordinary People Become Wealthy and How You Can Too."*

Sterne researched the stories of several millionaires for his book —and discovered they share the following traits:

Persistence: "You can't be a quitter. All millionaires know that if something good was easy to do, the entire world would probably be doing it. If you want to reap the benefits of success, be prepared to stick it out when other people might give up," said Sterne.

One millionaire who refused to give up on what others called an "impossible idea" was Charles Schwab, who founded the nation's largest discount stock brokerage.

Other brokerage houses were skeptical, but Schwab was convinced people would go for a no-frills trading service that sold stock with commission discounts averaging 50 percent. His perseverance paid off—and in 1983, he sold his company for $15 million.

Belief in their dreams and themselves. Millionaires believe "beyond a shadow of a doubt that they will become successful," said Sterne. "In order to become super successful, you must first not only believe in yourself, but must be able to visualize yourself becoming the success you desire."

Willingness to start small and set realistic targets. "Don't use the excuse that anything you do might be so small it isn't worth the effort," said Sterne.

Go ahead and set goals that are sky-high, but be sure to set

117

realistic steps to help you reach those goals. That way you can chart your progress—and watch the small victories add up to one big victory.

Also, be sure to set a timetable for achieving your goals. "There's no better way to galvanize yourself into action," said Sterne. "Having realistic goals and a timetable is certain to catapult you over the top."

One millionaire who started out small was Pierre de Beaumont. "He was 50 years old before he and his wife founded the Brookstone Co., a mail-order tool business, in their kitchen," said Sterne. "They began their company with $500—and later sold it for $9 million."

Willingness to delegate work. "Most millionaires begin as a one-man show, but eventually become more efficient by having others work for them," said Sterne. To follow their example, "learn to communicate well, be fair to your workers and delegate work that others can do while you pursue the big picture."

Choice of a field they truly enjoy. "Most successful people are that way because they enjoy what they're doing. The trick is to enjoy it so that it really doesn't seem like work," said Sterne.

Gary Gabrell, for example, turned his hobby into a million dollars. A pizzeria manager, Gabrell was also an enthusiastic games player. He became enthralled by an old Japanese game, called Pente, a cross between checkers and tick-tack-toe. Gabrell obtained a copyright on the name Pente and the design of the game board. Starting out with a borrowed $20,000, he sold 300 games in 1978—and went on to sell hundreds of thousands more.

—CLIFF BARR

In addition to books, we also produce cassette tape albums. Profit Ideas "Fast Start" distributors are able to buy wholesale or we dropship for them.

BECOME A "FAST START" BOOK DISTRIBUTOR AND HAVE RUSS VON HOELSCHER AS YOUR PERSONAL MARKETING CONSULTANT

Here's what you'll receive:

A Copy of 6 New Best-selling, Large, 6x9-Size, Soft-cover Books:

(1) *How to Achieve Total Success*—the revolutionary mind-science success manual. This powerful success book is changing lives worldwide.

(2) *Secrets of the Millionaires*—written by a millionaire for future millionaires.
All the secrets of obtaining great wealth in one big volume. Now you really can get rich!

(3) *Making Money for Yourself*—the best book available on how to start your own business and make a bundle of money!

(4) *Stay Home and Make Money*—the No. 1 home business manual. Loaded with today's best home business money plans.

(5) *Real Estate Wealth-Building Opportunities*—All the secrets of creating wealth in the real world monopoly game are here. Includes a master plan on how to pyramid a one thousand dollar investment into one million dollars!

(6) *How You Can Make a Fortune Selling Information by Mail*—Master strategies, techniques, tips and tricks on how to make mega-bucks selling information (books, reports, newsletters, tapes, etc.) by mail.

You'll also receive:

THE "FAST START" DEALERSHIP KIT:

► A copy of Russ von Hoelscher's start-up manual, *How to Make Big Money With Books*

► A subscription to the dealer's confidential *FAST START Newsletter*

► Camera-ready, result-getting ads and sales letters

► Updates on all new books, tapes, etc., available only to "FAST START" dealers.

► Free phone consultation with Russ, as often as you need it

JOIN NOW! Your total cost is only $69.95 (plus $4.20 sales tax for Californians only), and $5 for shipping costs. Call (619) 432-6913 and use your Mastercard/VISA, or send check or money order to: PROFIT IDEAS, Dept. FS, 254 E. Grand Avenue, Escondido, CA 92025. As soon as your order is received by phone or mail, the complete *"FAST START" kit* and copies of the 6 superb books will be promptly shipped to you. *(Your satisfaction is guaranteed or return everything within 30 days for a full refund.)*